CAPITAL MAGNET FUND

INTERIM IMPACT ASSESSMENT

CREATING AFFORDABLE HOMES FOR AMERICA

An impact assessment of the Capital Magnet Fund

COMMUNITY DEVELOPMENT FINANCIAL INSTITUTIONS FUND

U.S. DEPARTMENT OF THE TREASURY

MARCH 2014

TABLE OF CONTENTS

INTRODUCTION   3

EXECUTIVE SUMMARY   4

ABOUT THE CDFI FUND   7

ABOUT THE CAPITAL MAGNET FUND   9

FINDINGS   12

CONCLUSION   26

APPENDIX

APPENDIX 1: CAPITAL MAGNET FUND AWARDEES   27

APPENDIX 2: ABBREVIATIONS & ACRONYMS   34

APPENDIX 3: CAPITAL MAGNET FUND
AWARDEE EXAMPLES OF WORK   35

In recent years, a lack of access to affordable housing and other essential community development projects has led to an increased need for alternative and reliable sources of financing for projects that begin to fill this gap.

Congress helped to address the need for affordable housing when it passed the Housing and Economic Recovery Act (HERA)* on July 30, 2008, which authorized the creation of the Capital Magnet Fund (CMF) under the U.S. Department of the Treasury's Community Development Financial Institutions Fund (CDFI Fund). The current conservatorship of Fannie Mae and Freddie Mac led to the suspension of this funding. In response, Congress provided the Capital Magnet Fund with $80 million in appropriations for FY 2010 in order to jump-start the program.

Through the Capital Magnet Fund, the CDFI Fund provides competitively awarded grants to CDFIs and qualified nonprofit housing organizations. CMF awards finance affordable housing activities, as well as related economic development activities and community service facilities.

This report provides information about how Capital Magnet Fund awardees utilized this initial funding to provide affordable housing and vital economic development and community service facilities across the nation. From housing for our nation's seniors to wellness centers for low-income citizens, the Capital Magnet Fund is an effective investment. Awardees have leveraged the initial federal investment by 12 times through other public and private investment, already generating more than $1 billion of investment in affordable housing and associated community and economic development. Capital Magnet Fund awardees can play a key role in ensuring access to credit for both homebuyers and for providers of affordable rental housing.

Programs like the CDFI Fund's Capital Magnet Fund can help provide a sound financial investment in America's affordable housing stock in areas often left behind in a thriving economy.

*Public Law 110-289, Section 1339, 12 USC 4569.

EXECUTIVE SUMMARY

Access to affordable housing and other essential economic development and community services facilities has become an issue of critical importance in the United States. The Center for Housing Policy found that more than one in four renter households spent more than half of their income on housing. In most places, rents are rising faster than income.[1]

Through the Capital Magnet Fund, the CDFI Fund provides competitively awarded grants to CDFIs and qualified nonprofit housing organizations. CMF awards can be used to finance affordable housing activities as well as related economic development activities and community service facilities. Awardees utilize financing tools such as loan loss reserves, loan funds, risk-sharing loans, and loan guarantees to produce eligible activities within five years with aggregate costs that are at least 10 times the size of the award amount.

Congress provided the Capital Magnet Fund with $80 million in appropriations for FY 2010 in order to jump-start the program. Early results from this funding show that the Capital Magnet Fund is performing as intended. Capital Magnet Fund awardees either committed, started, or completed activities in 28 states, the District of Columbia, and Puerto Rico. This includes 189 development and preservation projects, as well as community and economic development projects, and 105 instances of assistance to homebuyers.

Through 2012, CMF awardees disbursed slightly over $62 million and committed the remainder, already producing over $1 billion in affordable housing and community and economic development projects. Additional leverage and production are expected as the remaining funds are disbursed, recovered, and reinvested.

Almost all of the CMF awardees used multiple sources of funding as leverage. On average, respondents used at least four different sources of funding for leverage with one CMF awardee using eight different sources of funding.

---

1. "Making the Mortgage Market Work for America's Families," Center for American Progress and the National Council of La Raza, http://www.americanprogress.org/wp-content/uploads/2013/06/AccessAffordHousing1.pdf, June 5, 2013.

Capital Magnet Fund awardees disbursed 78 percent of the funding awarded by the end of 2012, and 84 percent of the projects committed are already completed or partially completed. While awardees were able to use up to 5 percent of their awards for operations, they reported only using 2.5 percent to date for operations.

The Capital Magnet Fund is supporting almost 7,000 units, many of these for our nation's elderly, disabled Americans, homeless, veterans, and those most in need. The average federal CMF investment in these units was just $11,000 even though the average cost of the unit was $140,000, demonstrating the power of the leverage required through the Capital Magnet Fund.

Of the total CMF uses reported, 112 or 38 percent involve multi-family projects including new development and preservation (with and without rehabilitation). These projects received disbursements of $53 million of CMF awards and commitments for $14.5 million of CMF awards, which generated a total of $957 million of investment.

Of the single-family housing projects, 62 or 21 percent involve new development and preservation (with and without rehabilitation). These projects received disbursements for $3.4 million of CMF awards and commitments for $3.5 million of CMF awards, which generated a total of $54.5 million of investment.

Financial assistance to 105 homebuyers was another use of this funding. This assistance used $353,546 of CMF awards, which generated a total of $4.2 million of investment.

Fifteen community service and economic development projects were supported by CMF awardees ranging from business finance to child care to homeless counseling services to healthcare. These projects used $5.5 million of CMF awards, which generated a total of almost $53 million of investment.

RIVER SENIOR APARTMENTS
RENO, NEVADA
Idaho-Nevada CDFI, Inc.
See success story on page 102.

In total, Capital Magnet Fund awardees have already leveraged the initial awards by 12 times through other public and private investment. The result has been more than $1 billion of investment in affordable housing and associated community and economic development.

In addition, CMF awardees have started to recover their first investments and reinvest in other projects. Of the funding reinvested, 99.4 percent has been reinvested into affordable housing projects and .5 percent has been reinvested in community and economic development and revolving loan funds.

MCKINISTRY PLACE
DETROIT, MICHIGAN
Southwest Housing Solutions
Corporation

See success story on page 92.

ABOUT THE CDFI FUND

In 1994, the Community Development Financial Institutions Fund (CDFI Fund) was created for the purpose of promoting economic and community development through the investment in and assistance to Community Development Financial Institutions (CDFIs). The CDFI Fund supports these mission-driven financial institutions working on a local level that know their communities best.

CDFIs are specialized, community-based financial institutions that serve low-income people and organizations in economically distressed communities, often working in market niches that may be underserved by traditional financial institutions. CDFIs provide a unique and wide range of financial products and services. While the types of products made available are generally similar to those provided by mainstream financial institutions (such as mortgage financing for low-income and first-time homebuyers, small business lending, and lending for community facilities), CDFIs often lend to and make equity investments in markets that may not be served by mainstream financial institutions. In addition, CDFIs may offer rates and terms that are more flexible to low-income borrowers.

CDFIs also provide services that help ensure that credit is used effectively, such as technical assistance to small businesses and homebuying and credit counseling to consumers. CDFIs include depository institutions, such as community development banks and credit unions, and non-depository institutions, such as loan funds and venture capital funds.

Financial institutions that are certified by the CDFI Fund become eligible to apply for the CDFI Fund's comprehensive services— including monetary support and training to build organizational capacity. The CDFI Fund's awards are competitive and each of its programs provides CDFIs with the flexibility to determine the best use of limited federal resources in their communities. In addition to the Capital Magnet Fund, the CDFI Fund makes an impact through a wide range of innovative programs.

CDFI Program: Provides Financial Assistance and Technical Assistance awards to certified and emerging CDFIs to sustain and expand their services and to build their technical capacity.

2012 CDFI FUND RESULTS*

CDFI Program awardees reported:

- 4,102 businesses financed;
- 24,466 affordable housing units financed; and
- 25,618 jobs created or maintained.

New Markets Tax Credit allocatees:

- Increased by $5.5 billion the amount in loans and investments in low-income communities made possible under the New Markets Tax Credit Program, of which 70 percent were in severely distressed communities.
- Financed the development of $18.6 million worth of square feet of commercial real estate.
- Created or preserved 31,405 jobs.

BEA Program applicants increased by $432 million their investment in community development projects over their prior year's investment in these types of projects.

*Most recent year available.

New Markets Tax Credit Program (NMTC Program):
Provides investment allocation authority to certified Community Development Entities (CDEs), enabling investors to claim tax credits against their federal income taxes. The CDEs, in turn, use the capital raised to make loans and investments in low-income communities.

Bank Enterprise Award Program (BEA Program): Provides monetary awards to Federal Deposit Insurance Corporation insured banks for increasing their investments in low-income communities and/or in CDFIs.

CDFI Bond Guarantee Program: Guarantees bonds issued to support CDFIs that make loans for eligible community or economic development purposes. These bonds support CDFI lending by providing a source of long-term, patient capital.

Native Initiatives: Includes the Native American CDFI Assistance Program (NACA Program), which provides Financial Assistance and Technical Assistance awards to CDFIs serving Native communities to sustain and expand their services and to build their technical capacity; as well as training opportunities for Native CDFIs available as part of the CDFI Fund's Capacity Building Initiative.

Healthy Food Financing Initiative (HFFI): HFFI increases the availability of affordable, healthy foods in underserved urban and rural communities by helping overcome barriers to retailers of healthy food investing in economically distressed communities. Certified CDFIs with sound strategies for addressing the healthy food needs of communities can apply for grants to improve access to fresh food in low-income and underserved communities.

The CDFI Fund is helping to create economic opportunity in America's underserved communities and transforming the lives of the people who live and work there. Because investment decisions are made at the local level by CDFIs, financial products and investments target the community's greatest needs and opportunities.

Since the CDFI Fund was created in 1994, organizations have received over $1.8 billion in awards through the CDFI Program, BEA Program, NACA Program, Financial Education Counseling Pilot Program, and the Capital Magnet Fund, and $36.5 billion in New Markets Tax Credit investment allocation authority.

ZAPATA APARTMENTS
CHICAGO, ILLINOIS
Local Initiatives Support Corporation
See success story on page 70.

ABOUT THE CAPITAL MAGNET FUND

Congress passed and the President signed into law the Housing and Economic Recovery Act (HERA)[2] on July 30, 2008, establishing the Capital Magnet Fund (CMF) under the U.S. Department of the Treasury's Community Development Financial Institutions Fund (CDFI Fund).

Through the Capital Magnet Fund, Congress sought to enlist highly successful certified community development financial institutions (CDFIs) and nonprofit housing developers to address challenges in the housing market, including the lack of affordable housing, increasing foreclosures, and neighborhood stability.

HERA authorized the creation of this competitive grant program to attract additional capital for affordable housing primarily for low-income households, and to spur associated community and economic development activities with the objective of revitalizing low-income communities and underserved rural areas. Through the Capital Magnet Fund, the CDFI Fund provides Financial Assistance awards to certified CDFIs as well as to nonprofit affordable housing organizations.

Funding for CMF was to come from mandatory contributions by Fannie Mae and Freddie Mac; however, their ensuing conservatorship led to the suspension of this funding mechanism. In response, Congress provided the Capital Magnet Fund with $80 million in appropriations for FY 2010 in order to jump-start the program.

The CDFI Fund received 230 applications from organizations serving 49 states, the District of Columbia, and Puerto Rico. The amount requested totaled more than $1 billion in grants. On October 10, 2010, the CDFI Fund announced $80 million in Capital Magnet Fund awards to 23 CDFIs and nonprofit housing developers. Of the 23 CMF awardees, 13 were nonprofit housing organizations; nine were CDFIs; and one was a Tribal housing authority.

Eligibility Requirements: To be eligible for a Capital Magnet Fund award, an applicant must be certified as a CDFI by the CDFI Fund, have an application for CDFI certification pending with the CDFI Fund, or be a nonprofit organization that has the development or management of affordable housing as one of its principal purposes.

"According to projections of the U.S. Census Bureau, the national population will likely increase from 310 million in 2010 to nearly 334 million in 2020. By mid-century, the Census Bureau projects that the U.S. population will exceed 400 million. As the population grows, the demand for new and upgraded housing will grow as well. The production of new housing units as well as the preservation and renovation of existing units, both owner-occupied and rental, should be a major dynamic force in the overall national economy."

BIPARTISAN POLICY CENTER
"HOUSING AMERICA'S FUTURE: NEW DIRECTIONS FOR NATIONAL POLICY"
February 2013

2. Public Law 110-289, Section 1339, 12 USC 4569.

Eligible Uses: An applicant can apply for a Capital Magnet Fund award to support financing related to certain types of development activities. These include:

- Affordable housing activities including the preservation, rehabilitation, or purchase of affordable housing for low-income communities.

- Economic development activities and community service facilities including the development of physical structures for local businesses, provided that these activities are part of a concerted strategy for community revitalization that includes affordable housing activities. Examples of community service facilities include day care centers, workforce development centers, and healthcare clinics, among others.

An organization can use its Capital Magnet Fund award for a wide range of purposes:

- To provide loan loss reserves;

- To capitalize a revolving loan fund;

- To capitalize an affordable housing fund;

- To capitalize a fund to support economic development activities or community service facilities;

- To provide risk-sharing loans;

- To provide loan guarantees; or

- To support operations pertaining to the administration of the Capital Magnet Fund award.

Awardees can use no more than 30 percent of their Capital Magnet Fund awards for economic development activities and community service facilities, and no more than 5 percent of their awards for operations.

Awardees are required to leverage the Capital Magnet Fund award with other sources of capital. The leveraged amount is required to be at least 10 times the amount of the award. Awardees must commit Capital Magnet Fund awards for use within two years after the CDFI Fund allocates the awards, and must complete projects within five years.

CAPITAL MAGNET FUND AWARDEES

Green denotes headquarters of Capital Magnet Fund awardees;
blue indicates Capital Magnet Fund projects; and red indicates
national foreclosure quintiles.

CMF Awardees

CMF Projects

Foreclosure Quintiles 2010, HUD

☐ No data

0

1

2

3

4

5

FINDINGS

The CDFI Fund annually collects performance data submitted by awardees through the CDFI Fund's data collection system known as the Community Investment Impact System (CIIS). As part of compliance requirements, award recipients under the CDFI Fund's Capital Magnet Fund are required to submit information through CIIS after the close of their fiscal year. This includes a CMF Activities Report, as well as an A-133 audit and financial report.

The CMF Activities Report looks at awardees in detail, tracking loans or investments made, including borrower and project addresses, borrower socioeconomic characteristics, loan or investment terms, repayment status, and community development outcomes. The A-133 audit and the financial report help the CDFI Fund to gain an understanding of and test the awardee's internal controls, and determine whether the awardee complied with laws, regulations, and the provisions of the Capital Magnet Fund Program.

In July 2013, the CDFI Fund finalized Capital Magnet Fund awardees' first performance reporting. For the first two years of investment activities (2011-2012), Capital Magnet Fund awardees either committed, started, or completed activities in 28 states, the District of Columbia, and Puerto Rico. This includes 189 housing development and preservation projects, as well as community and economic development projects, and assistance to 105 homebuyers. It should be noted that these are initial results.

As a result of the affordable housing and community and economic development provided by CMF awardees, 5,456 construction jobs were created and 315 full-time jobs were created or maintained. To benchmark the CMF job impacts, the estimate is compared to a study by the Bipartisan Policy Center, which found that the construction of a typical 100-unit, multi-family development creates 80 jobs directly (through construction) or indirectly (through the supply chain), plus another 42 jobs in a range of local occupations as a result of construction workers spending their wages.[3]

CMF RESULTS THROUGH YEAR-END 2012

Leverage — 1:12*

Total number of projected affordable homes — **6,803**

    Number of owner-occupied homes financed — **502**

    Number of affordable rental homes financed — **6,301**

Average CMF award investment per home — **$11,000**

Total average cost per home (based on CMF funding and all other funding leveraged) — **$140,000**

Number of full-time jobs created or maintained — **315**

Number of construction jobs — **5,456**

Number of development and preservation projects (including community and economic development) — **189**

Assistance to homebuyers — **105**

*Does not include leverage from reinvestment of funds.

---

3. "Housing America's Future: New Directions for National Policy," Bipartisan Policy Center, http://bipartisanpolicy.org/sites/default/files/BPC_Housing%20Report_web_0.pdf, February 2013.

Similar economic benefits apply to single-family construction as well as renovation activity. Construction and renovation also generate tax revenue for states and localities, helping to support the provision of essential public services.

Award Investment

As of year-end 2012, Capital Magnet Fund awardees have disbursed 78 percent of the funding awarded, or $62,314,175 and committed but not disbursed $17,685,825. CMF awardees must complete projects within five years. As shown below, 84 percent of the projects reported are already completed or partially completed.

Project Status	Number of Projects [4]	Disbursements or Commitments to Date	Total Project Costs
Committed and disbursed	17	$10,702,740	$195,987,904
Completed	191	$24,278,493	$318,932,733
Partially Completed	57	$27,332,940	$433,965,302
Sub-Total	**265**	**$62,314,175**	**$948,885,939**
Committed, not yet disbursed	29	$17,685,825	$120,280,846
Total	**294**	**$80,000,000**	**$1,069,166,785**

Use of Funds

Capital Magnet Fund awardees can use their awards for a wide range of tools for affordable housing. These include loan loss reserves; revolving loan funds; affordable housing funds; funds to support economic development activities or community service facilities; risk-sharing loans; loan guarantees; or to support operations pertaining to the administration of the Capital Magnet Fund award.

Through 2012, CMF awardees had disbursed slightly over $62 million of their CMF awards and committed another $17.6 million which has produced a total project benefit of over $1 billion in 189 affordable housing and community and economic development projects disbursed and 105 instances of assistance to homebuyers.

While awardees were able to use up to 5 percent of their awards for operations, they reported only using 2.5 percent to date for operations.

4. Projects include homebuyers assistance.

RICE SILK MILL
BOSTON, MASSACHUSETTS
Massachusetts Housing Partnership

See success story on page 82.

In addition to direct financing of affordable housing and community and economic development projects, CMF awardees provided loan guarantees, revolving loan funds, and loan loss reserve funds to better leverage the awards.

Most notably, CMF awardees have started to receive repayments of their early financings and have begun investing in other projects. Almost all reinvestment so far has been invested back into affordable housing projects at 99.4 percent; .5 percent has been reinvested in community and economic development and revolving loan funds.

PRESTON PLACE
BALTIMORE, MARYLAND
The Reinvestment Fund
See success story on page 76.

Purpose	Amount	Percentage by Purpose
Investment (Disbursements)		
Affordable Housing Loans	$35,582,176	57.13%
Community/Economic Development Loans	$3,731,168	6.10%
Loan Guarantees	$8,890,755	14.52%
Loan Loss Reserve	$114,856	0.19%
Revolving Loan Fund	$11,218,509	18.33%
Not Defined	$1,674,153	2.74%
Operations (as a share of all awards)		
Awardee's Operations	$2,000,356	2.5%
Reinvestment		
Affordable Housing Loans	$16,700,027	99.40%
Community/Economic Development Loans	$32,000	0.2%
Revolving Loan Fund	$56,000	0.3%

Affordable Housing Activity

Multi-family projects, including new development and preservation (with and without rehabilitation), used the vast majority of CMF dollars. Awardees reported disbursement of slightly over $53 million and a commitment of over $17.9 million of CMF funds ($957 million total project cost). Rental developers need financing to build properties and property owners need it to buy, repair, rehabilitate, and preserve rental housing. The cost and availability of credit to support the rental sector is important to maintaining a supply of rental housing adequate to meet the demand for it, and because rental markets are competitive; credit costs and availability influence the rents that landlords charge.[5]

Single-family residences, including new development and preservation (with and without rehabilitation) made up 21 percent of the reported CMF activities. These projects received disbursements for $3.4 million of CMF awards and commitments for nearly $3.5 million, which generated a total of $54.5 million of investment. CMF awardees also reported 15 community and/or economic development activities (including business finance, child care services, homeless counseling services, and healthcare). These projects used $5.5 million of CMF awards, which generated a total of almost $53 million of investment.

Finally, home purchase assistance was another use of funds, making up slightly less than 1 percent of total funding. Home purchase assistance includes down-payment assistance and counseling. Of the total completed CMF uses reported, 105 or 36 percent were for financial assistance to homebuyers. Awardees supported homebuyers assistance with $353,546 of CMF funds, which generated a total of $4.2 million of investment.

According to the Center for American Progress and the National Council of La Raza, "Research indicates that low- and moderate-income borrowers and other underserved populations sometimes considered too risky to finance can be high-performing customers when placed in sustainable, affordable mortgages. The report further suggests that people who have stable, decent homes have an easier time holding down a job and their children do better in school. There is also evidence that a mix of quality housing options helps make communities more vibrant, diverse, and livable."[6]

DELTA RIVER SENIOR VILLAGE
LANSING, MICHIGAN
Volunteers of America
National Services
See success story on page 96.

5. "Housing America's Future: New Directions for National Policy," Bipartisan Policy Center, http://bipartisanpolicy.org/sites/default/files/BPC_Housing%20Report_web_0.pdf, February 2013.

6. "Window of Opportunity Preserving Affordable Rental House," The John D. and Catherine T. MacArthur Foundation, Chicago, IL, November 2007.

COMMUNITY/ECONOMIC DEVELOPMENT

Number of Projects: **15**
Share: **5%**
Disbursements to Date: **$5,511,526**
Commitments to Date: **$0**
Total Project Costs (including Commitments): **$52,993,198**

MULTI-FAMILY - NEW DEVELOPMENT & PRESERVATIONS (WITH AND WITHOUT REHABILITATION)

Number of Projects: **112**
Share: **38%**
Disbursements to Date: **$53,031,850**
Commitments to Date: **$14,521,412**
Total Project Costs (including Commitments): **$957,435,939**

SINGLE FAMILY - NEW DEVELOPMENT & PRESERVATIONS (WITH AND WITHOUT REHABILITATION)

Number of Projects: **62**
Share: **21%**
Disbursements to Date: **$3,434,365**
Commitments to Date: **$17,988,542**
Total Project Costs (including Commitments): **$54,504,799**

HOME PURCHASE ASSISTANCE (EACH HOME PURCHASE ASSISTANCE IS COUNTED AS AN INDIVIDUAL PROJECT)

Number of Projects: **105**
Share: **36%**
Disbursements to Date: **$336,434**
Commitments to Date: **$17,112**
Total Project Costs (including Commitments): **$4,232,849**

MCKINISTRY PLACE
ANCHORAGE, ALASKA
Volunteers of America
National Services
See success story on page 40.

Community and Economic Development Activity

Capital Magnet Fund awards are distinctive in that awardees can complement affordable housing with economic development activities and community service facilities. Eligible activities include the development of physical structures for local businesses, as well as community service facilities, provided that these activities are part of a concerted strategy for community revitalization that includes affordable housing activities. Since the Capital Magnet Fund is first and foremost an affordable housing program, community and economic development activities by awardees are limited to no more than 30 percent of the CMF award. In aggregate, less than 10 percent of overall CMF funds have been used for community and economic development.

CMF awardees reported a variety of economic development activities and the creation of community service facilities. The most common use was for multi-service facilities (60 percent of projects reported) followed by healthcare facilities (27 percent of the projects reported). Economic development activities represented 9 percent of funding distributed to date.

One example is a project by Forward Community Investments, which used part of its CMF award for the expansion of a dental facility in Dodgeville, Wisconsin. The facility now includes a 4,100 square foot dental clinic with eight patient treatment rooms, a waiting room reception area, and offices to provide services for low-income families from across Iowa County. It primarily serves people who are on Medicaid, and other low-income people are served on a sliding scale. In 2012 alone, the dental facility helped almost 1,400 patients.

Another example is the Gilroy Sobrato Apartments, a 26-studio apartment building of permanent housing for the chronically homeless by CMF awardee, South County Housing Corporation. The apartment amenities include a community room and conference rooms for residents to meet with their caseworkers and social service providers. Each resident receives a full spectrum of physical health, mental health, addiction recovery, and job training/search services.

The Low Income Investment Fund (LIIF) provided the Colorado Coalition for the Homeless (CCH), a leading developer and manager of mixed use-supportive housing and service facilities in Colorado, with a $500,000 tenant improvement loan for the West End Health Center in Denver.

The West End Health Center, a 7,400 square-foot facility co-located with a 101-unit, mixed-used affordable housing development, provides a host of services including primary health care, mental health care, substance treatment counseling, pharmacy and nursing services, and patient education. The clinic is projected to employ eight full-time employees and serve 1,200 Medicaid-qualified clients in its first year.

The 100 percent affordable housing development, financed separately, includes 50 supportive housing units for homeless individuals and families. The new clinic will cater to the 50 supportive units, as well as families in the surrounding community. LIIF's financing, which included a $58,000 credit enhancement from the Capital Magnet Fund, helped CCH complete the build out of the health clinic.

Another CMF awardee, The Community Builders, combined affordable housing with retail at the Shops and Lofts at 47 in Chicago's historic Bronzeville neighborhood (slated for completion in 2014). A Walmart Neighborhood Market will be the anchor commercial tenant with a 41,000 square-foot store that will provide residents of the neighborhood with greater access to jobs and fresh food—both long-standing issues in the traditionally underserved community. The $46.5 million complex is the first commercial and residential development in the area in more than 50 years.

CARDINAL LANE CONDOMINIUMS
HOPKINTON, RHODE ISLAND
Women's Development
Corporation

See success story on page 116.

Project	Number	Disbursements to Date	Total Project Costs
Business	1	$1,386,186	$12,487,718
Child Care	1	$64,750	$777,000
Healthcare	4	$767,736	$14,058,700
Multi-Service/Other	9	$3,292,854	$25,669,780
Total	15	$5,511,526	$52,993,198

Capital Magnet Fund Awardee Survey

In addition to the information collected through CIIS, on August 28, 2013, the CDFI Fund sent a brief survey to Capital Magnet Fund awardees. In conducting this five-question, voluntary survey, the CDFI Fund sought to collect information from Capital Magnet Fund awardees to provide more insight into the use of funds awarded.

The CDFI Fund received a 100 percent response rate from awardees to the survey. The respondents were:

- Abode Communities
- Century Housing Corporation
- Forward Community Investments
- Great Lakes Capital Fund Nonprofit Housing Corporation
- Habitat for Humanity International
- Hope Enterprise Corporation
- Idaho-Nevada Community Development Financial Institution
- Local Initiatives Support Corporation
- Low Income Investment Fund
- Massachusetts Housing Partnership
- New Hampshire Community Loan Fund, Inc.
- Northwest Real Estate Capital Corp.
- Ohio Capital Finance Corporation
- PathStone Corporation
- Rural Community Assistance Corporation
- San Carlos Housing Authority
- South County Housing Corporation
- Southwest Housing Solutions
- The Community Builders, Inc.
- The Reinvestment Fund, Inc.
- Volunteers of America National Services
- Western Community Housing, Inc.
- Women's Development Corporation

GILROY SOBRATO APARTMENTS
GILROY, CALIFORNIA
South County Housing Corporation

See success story on page 48.

Question 1: What were your sources of leverage (e.g., bank loans, foundation grants, etc.)? Please list all that apply and if possible the percentage used from the different sources of leverage.

All respondents (except two that used their own equity exclusively for leverage) used multiple sources of funding as leverage. The most common source of leverage was a wide variety of other federal funding, such as HOME Funds and USDA's Rural Development 502 loans.

A large percentage of respondents (48 percent) leveraged CMF funding with investments based on Low Income Housing Tax Credits. This was followed closely by funding from banks with 43 percent of respondents using that source.

Other sources of note include reduced or deferred developer fees, foundations, and donations from individuals and religious organizations.

On average, respondents used at least four different sources of funding for leverage, with one respondent using eight different sources of funding.

"The Capital Magnet Fund has been a valuable tool for the Low Income Investment Fund (LIIF) in providing gap-filling capital for complex transactions with multiple investors. LIIF's CMF-supported projects have included a range of additional capital providers, including public agencies, banks, foundations, a real estate investment trust, developers, and other community development financial institutions."

NANCY O. ANDREWS
PRESIDENT AND CEO
Low Income Investment Fund

Funding Source	Respondents that used source	
	Number	Percentage
Other Federal funding including Neighborhood Stabilization Program; HOME Funds; Rural Development 502 loans; HUD Section 202; CDBG; Federal Home Loan Bank; NeighborWorks; and New Markets Tax Credits	17	74%
Low Income Housing Tax Credit investors	11	48%
Banks	10	43%
State and local subsidies (e.g., tax credits)	8	35%
Developer fees (and deferred fees)	6	26%
Foundations	6	26%
Individual and religious donations	6	26%
Own equity	5	22%
Other investor equity and private sources	3	13%
CDFI loan pool	2	8%
Corporate sponsorships/donations	1	4%
Nonprofit investor	1	4%
Real estate investment trust	1	4%
Retail revenue	1	4%
Self-Help Land Loan	1	4%

Note that respondents could provide more than one answer.

BRODERICK-MURRAY APARTMENTS
DETROIT, MICHIGAN
Southwest Housing Solutions
Corporation

See success story on page 86.

Question 2: Did you combine economic development with housing? If so, what types of projects were included? Of the total projects, how many included economic development?

Of all Capital Magnet Fund awardees, 39 percent (9 respondents) reported that they did combine community or economic development with housing. The most predominant use was for development that combined affordable housing with commercial space. A wide variety of social services were provided from homeless counseling services to healthcare.

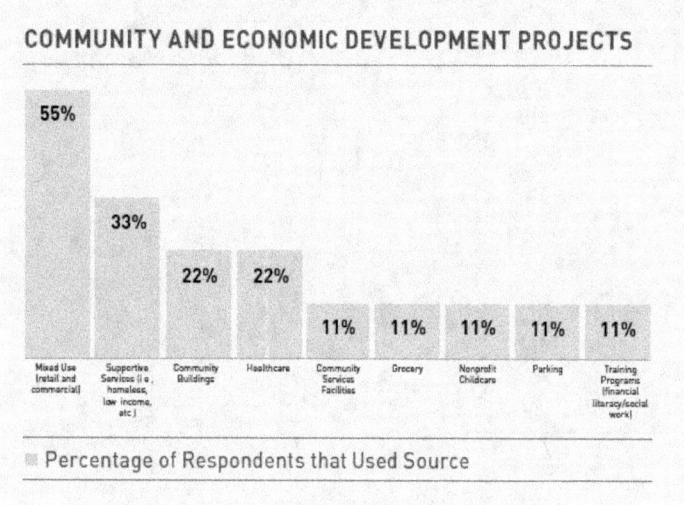

COMMUNITY AND ECONOMIC DEVELOPMENT PROJECTS

55%	Mixed Use (retail and commercial)
33%	Supportive Services (i.e., homeless, low income, etc.)
22%	Community Buildings
22%	Healthcare
11%	Community Services Facilities
11%	Grocery
11%	Nonprofit Childcare
11%	Parking
11%	Training Programs (financial literacy/social work)

■ Percentage of Respondents that Used Source

Note that responders could provide more than one answer.

"We funded two economic development projects in rural New Hampshire. One is a nonprofit child care center that serves low-income people in Winchester, New Hampshire, permitting parents to work. The other project is part of a multiple use revitalization development in Keene, New Hampshire, with facilities designed for nonprofit organizations that serve low-income people in the region."

JULIANA EADES
PRESIDENT
New Hampshire Community Loan Fund

Question 3: If you have used all your initial Capital Magnet Fund award funding, have you reinvested the funding into other projects? If so, please describe the types of projects. Please provide one or two examples.

Of all Capital Magnet Fund awardees, 74 percent (17 respondents) reported that they have committed all their Capital Magnet Fund awards to affordable housing projects and associated community or economic development; 26 percent (six respondents) stated that they have either not used all of their awards yet or have not begun reinvesting the funding into other projects. Capital Magnet Fund awardees have reinvested $16.8 million as of year-end 2012. Of the funding reinvested, 99.4 percent has been reinvested into affordable housing projects; .5 percent in community and economic development and revolving loan funds.

"We have reinvested our Capital Magnet Fund award into four additional projects that are located throughout California. All of the projects are deeply affordable to tenants with incomes at or below 60 percent of the area median income. One project will be developed in South Lake Tahoe in Northern California and will create 48 affordable homes to low-income families in the area. Another project is an existing affordable housing development that utilized our financing and Capital Magnet Funds to acquire and rehabilitate 129 affordable units for low-income families in Colton, California."

AARON WOOLER
SENIOR VICE PRESIDENT
Century Housing Corporation

Question 4: Did you fund projects with Capital Magnet Fund award funding that would not have been possible without the award? In other words, did you use the Capital Magnet Fund award for hard-to-finance projects?

All 23 Capital Magnet Fund awardees reported that they funded projects that would not have been possible without the Capital Magnet Fund award and for hard-to-finance projects.

CMF awardees leveraged their funding to provide bridge loans and gap financing for projects that otherwise could not have been accomplished through ordinary financing methods. Examples of hard-to-finance projects given were the preservation of 48 units of affordable housing and the new development of 140 affordable apartments. It also enabled a nonprofit developer to acquire and preserve affordable housing and was used for a hard-to-finance center for sexual and domestic abuse in Wisconsin. The most common answers to the question were as follows:

Financing Use	Number of Respondents
Gap financing/bridge loan/loan guarantees	8
Allowed to increase loan limit; reduce interest rate; expand risk profile	3
Helped obtain other funding (FHLB; banks)	3
Helped continuing projects in tough economy	2
To keep up with Low Income Housing Tax Credit demand	2
HUD section 8 housing	1

"While Low Income Housing Tax Credit investor equity pays for a large portion of our projects' total costs, if we did not have the Capital Magnet Fund award to bridge the financing gap, the projects would not have been possible because traditional borrowing and lending of money is virtually nonexistent on tribal trust land."

RONALD BONI
DIRECTOR
San Carlos Housing Authority

Question 5: In general, how useful was/is the funding you received from the Capital Magnet Fund?

All 23 Capital Magnet Fund awardees stated that the funding was extremely useful. Three Capital Magnet Fund awardees stated that the funds helped to strengthen their balance sheets to increase their ability to secure other capital from private financial institutions.

Six Capital Magnet Fund awardees (26 percent) stated that the flexibility of the award was key to funding projects. Without the funding, the awardees would not have been able to fund the transactions out of their general loan fund; the funds enabled awardees to continue to serve more and more families in need.

Three Capital Magnet Fund awardees (13 percent) stated that the funding helped them to extend their reach; increase the impact of the dollars lent by allowing them to offer more favorable interest rates; and allowed them to go into hard-to-reach rural and urban markets.

Seven Capital Magnet Fund awardees (30 percent) reported that the funds were vital for bridge loans and time-sensitive funding such as Low Income Housing Tax Credit, HUD Section 8, and USDA section 515 housing projects. According to a report by the Center for American Progress and the National Council of La Raza, "To preserve older affordable rental housing, developers often need financing to acquire as well as renovate the properties."[7]

And finally three Capital Magnet Fund awardees (13 percent) provided examples of being able to finance specific projects: 192 new affordable senior housing units (Idaho Nevada CDFI); the building of 31 new units and renovating 50 existing units, creating a lasting change for the community on reservation lands (San Carlos Housing Authority); and 80 units of housing that would have been on hold without the Capital Magnet Fund award (Women's Development Corporation).

"The Capital Magnet Fund was absolutely critical for us to be able expand our lending relationships with area banks—we've had two successive years of record financing for affordable housing properties, and we wouldn't have had the capital to meet this high demand for funding without the resources of the Capital Magnet Fund."

MARK A. CURTISS
MANAGING DIRECTOR
Massachusetts Housing Partnership

7. Id. at 1.

CONCLUSION

According to the paper, "Housing Policy in the United States," the housing sector is one of the largest components of the U.S. economy and has consistently accounted for more than one fifth of the nation's gross domestic product, including 5 percent for residential construction and remodeling, 11 percent for rental payments and homeowner expenditures, and 7 percent for utilities, appliances, and home furnishings.[8] Access to affordable housing and other critical community development projects have never been more vital to the United States.

Capital Magnet Fund awards are being used successfully to finance affordable housing activities as well as related economic development activities and community service facilities. CMF awardees are utilizing financing tools such as loan loss reserves, loan funds, risk-sharing loans, and loan guarantees to produce activities in communities most in need of affordable housing.

The Capital Magnet Fund has increased the number of safe, affordable housing units in America by almost 7,000 units, many of these for our nation's elderly, disabled Americans, homeless, and those most in need. The average CMF investment in these units was just $11,000 even though the average total cost of the unit was $140,000. This is the power of leverage required through the Capital Magnet Fund.

Awardees have already leveraged the initial CMF investment by 12 times through other public and private investment, creating more than $1 billion of investment in affordable housing and associated community and economic development. Capital Magnet Fund awardees can and will play a key role in ensuring access to credit for both homebuyers and for providers of affordable rental housing.

> "For projects that traditional financing was not available and city funding was not permitted to purchase the land, our Capital Magnet Fund loans allowed a stalled pipeline of Low Income Housing Tax Credit projects to be built for very deserving residents in needed neighborhoods. The impact of loaning CMF funds into the affordable housing sector at a time when local subsidies are hard to find, residents and communities benefited tremendously from our Capital Magnet Fund award through the revitalization of older neighborhoods, creation of jobs, and providing housing for lower-income families and seniors in desperate need of quality affordable housing. The CMF funding by the CDFI Fund for affordable housing projects could not have come at a better time."

GRAHAM ESPLEY-JONES
PRESIDENT
Western Community
Housing, Inc.

8. Schwartz, Alex F., "Housing policy in the United States," New York: Routledge, 2013.

APPENDIX 1: CAPITAL MAGNET FUND AWARDEES

Abode Communities: Founded 41-years ago as a volunteer organization of architects, Abode Communities has provided comprehensive architectural services and technical assistance to more than 500 community groups, including permanent and sustainable affordable housing projects, homeless shelters, child care centers, health clinics, and senior centers. Abode Communities' mission is to open new doors in people's lives through creative and responsible design, development, and operation of service-enhanced affordable housing. Abode Communities' specific strength is building sustainable, multi-family affordable housing to address the needs of Southern California's large workforce, low-income families, seniors, and individuals with special needs.

Century Housing Corporation (Century): Century finances affordable housing developments throughout California. From bridge loans to acquisition loans to construction loans, Century has worked for more than 15 years to provide tax-credit developers and infill developers with innovative loans and responsive service. Century invests in homes and communities so that low-income individuals and families may have a dignified living environment, achieve economic independence, and enjoy healthful and vital places to live and work. Century believes that a just society provides safe, quality, and affordable housing for all.

Forward Community Investments (FCI): FCI transforms communities by supporting projects and programs that focus on affordable housing, job creation, economic development, and basic social services. Whether it's through one-on-one advising or workshops, FCI works with nonprofit managers to assess their organization's financial and organizational condition and help them appreciate their strengths and opportunities and manage areas of financial weakness. This is all done for the purpose of increasing programmatic effectiveness and expanding the opportunity for greater social impact. FCI offers a variety of workshops, webinars, and one-on-one advising that are designed to build its clients' capacity, grow their financial effectiveness, and improve their social impact. FCI provides money and expert advisory services to nonprofit organizations serving communities most in need. Since 1994, Forward Community Investments has lent more than $25 million to nonprofits across Wisconsin. These loans have created and sustained more than 1,200 units of affordable homes, provided affordable childcare for 1,500 children, and created or retained 3,100 jobs.

Great Lakes Capital Fund Nonprofit Housing Corporation (GLCF):
The Great Lakes Capital Fund Nonprofit Housing Corporation
was established in 1993 and operates in Michigan, Indiana,
Illinois, Upstate New York, and Wisconsin. GLCF is a designated
CDFI that invests chiefly in housing created through the federal
Low Income Housing Tax Credit. GLCF also provides access
to other financial resources and technical assistance through
its lending arm, Capital Fund Services, and is a Fannie Mae
delegated underwriter and servicer. GLCF's "One Stop Shopping"
program enables developers to access permanent debt financing,
construction lending, equity investment, technical assistance,
and predevelopment loans through a single proposal. GLCF
also operates a New Market Tax Credit portfolio and sources
investments in state historic and brownfield tax credits.

Habitat for Humanity International (HFHI): HFHI is a nonprofit,
faith-based housing organization. Founded in 1976, HFHI's mission
is to build simple, decent, affordable housing in partnership
with people in need. Since 1997, its Flexible Capital Access
Program (FlexCAP) and its predecessor program have generated
approximately $91 million in loans for over 200 U.S. HFHI
affiliates, providing funding for approximately 2,000 new Habitat
homes. HFHI has more than 1,500 local affiliates in the United
States and more than 70 national organizations around the world.

Hope Enterprise Corporation (HOPE): Hope is a private, nonprofit
CDFI that provides commercial financing, mortgage loans and
technical assistance to support businesses, entrepreneurs,
homebuyers, and community development projects. HOPE's
mission is to strengthen communities, build assets, and improve
lives of people in economically distressed areas of Arkansas,
Louisiana, Mississippi, and Tennessee. Since 1994, HOPE has
generated over $1.7 billion in financing for entrepreneurs,
homebuyers, and community development projects, and assisted
more than 400,000 individuals in low-income communities
throughout the Mid-South.

**Idaho-Nevada Community Development Financial Institution,
Inc.:** The Idaho-Nevada CDFI, Inc. was founded in 1999 to
provide financing to small businesses and affordable housing
entrepreneurs in the Intermountain West. The Idaho-Nevada
CDFI, Inc. has a primary market of Idaho and Nevada. However,
on a case-by-case basis it will consider projects in other western
states having distinct community development impact. Idaho-

Nevada CDFI, Inc. provides financing to both for-profit and nonprofit organizations. The CDFI has found that a combination of targeted, project-specific technical assistance and low-interest financing is required by nonprofit housing developers and small businesses to move projects along in a timely manner and ensure a high-quality viable project.

Local Initiatives Support Corporation (LISC): LISC is dedicated to helping community residents transform distressed neighborhoods into healthy and sustainable communities of choice and opportunity — good places to work, do business, and raise children. For almost three decades, LISC has connected local organizations and community leaders with resources to revitalize neighborhoods and improve quality of life. The LISC model assembles private and public resources and directs it to locally-defined priorities. Its unique structure enables local organizations to access national resources and expertise, and its funding partners to leverage their investment and achieve an impact that is truly remarkable. LISC is a national organization with a community focus. LISC's program staff is based in every city and many of the rural areas where LISC-supported community development takes shape. In collaboration with local community development groups, LISC staff help identify priorities and challenges, delivering the most appropriate support to meet local needs.

Low Income Investment Fund (LIIF): As a leading national CDFI, LIIF invests capital in low-income people and communities. Since its founding in 1984, LIIF has invested $1.3 billion in projects serving highly distressed neighborhoods. Through its financing and technical assistance, LIIF has served 1.4 million people and generated $25 billion in family and societal benefits.

Massachusetts Housing Partnership (MHP): The Massachusetts Housing Partnership is a statewide public nonprofit affordable housing organization that works in concert with the Governor and the state Department of Housing and Community Development to help increase the supply of affordable housing in Massachusetts. MHP was established in 1985 to increase the state's overall rate of housing production and find creative new solutions to address the need for affordable housing. In 1990, the state legislature took that premise to heart, becoming the first and only state in the nation to pass an interstate banking act that requires companies that acquire Massachusetts banks to make funds available to MHP for affordable housing. MHP's Community Housing Initiatives team works with communities, local housing groups, and nonprofit developers on local housing initiatives. Using its bank-funded loan pool, MHP provides long-term financing for the development and preservation of affordable rental housing.

New Hampshire Community Loan Fund: The New Hampshire Community Loan Fund provides the financing and educational tools people need to own homes, have quality jobs and child care, and become financially independent. Established in 1983 in Concord, New Hampshire, the New Hampshire Community Loan Fund was one of the first CDFIs in the United States. The New Hampshire Community Loan Fund has loaned more than $150 million to thousands of New Hampshire individuals, organizations, and employers. Nearly every project is a collaboration with a variety of donors and lenders, including banks, credit unions, as well as other business, nonprofit, and government partners.

Northwest Real Estate Capital Corp.: Northwest Real Estate Capital Corp. was formed in 1999. It is a regional tax-exempt affordable housing preservation company headquartered in Boise, Idaho. Since inception, the company has acquired, financed, rehabilitated, preserved, and manages over $130 million of new and existing multi-family housing in the Northwest, benefiting low-income families, the elderly, and disabled persons with incomes below 40 percent of the adjusted median income. The company's preservation activities include most types of federally regulated housing, including HUD Section 8, 202, 236, 811, Home, Section 42, USDA Section 515, and related affordable housing programs.

Ohio Capital Finance Corporation (OCFC): OCFC is the lending arm of the Ohio Capital Corporation for Housing (OCCH). OCFC was created in 2002 to further expand OCCH's predevelopment lending activities. In May 2010, OCFC, with the assistance of the Ohio Housing Finance Agency, created the Ohio Preservation Loan Fund. The Preservation Loan Fund is designed to provide developers and owners of existing affordable housing with the tools necessary to allow the refinance and transfer of ownership while continuing the use of ongoing rental subsidies. OCFC is using its Capital Magnet Fund award to leverage investor equity in affordable housing transactions. OCFC offers products that are necessary, especially for nonprofit developers, and that generally are not otherwise available. OCFC lending permits developers to gain site control, engage engineering and environmental studies, hire architects and attorneys, conduct market studies, package projects for construction and permanent financing, as well as the acquisition of land and/or buildings for affordable housing development.

PathStone Corporation: PathStone Corporation is a nonprofit organization established in 1969 that has developed, improved, or acquired more than 10,000 units of affordable housing in five states and Puerto Rico. PathStone is a regional community development and human service organization providing services to farm workers, low-income families, and economically depressed communities.

Rural Community Assistance Corporation (RCAC): RCAC is a nonprofit organization that provides technical assistance, training, and financing so rural communities achieve their goals and visions. Headquartered in West Sacramento, California, RCAC's employees serve rural communities in 13 western states, plus the western Pacific. RCAC's work encompasses a wide range of services including technical assistance and training for environmental infrastructure, affordable housing development, economic and leadership development, and community development finance. These services are available to a variety of communities and organizations including communities with populations of fewer than 50,000, other nonprofit groups, and tribal organizations.

San Carlos Housing Authority (SCHA): The San Carlos Housing Authority is the tribal-designated housing entity of the San Carlos Apache Tribe in Southeastern Arizona. The SCHA was established in 1961, and is the only provider of affordable housing on the San Carlos Reservation. The SCHA received the 2012 Most Valuable Partner Award from the U.S. Department of Housing and Urban Development for the 220 new homes that have been built within the San Carlos Apache Indian Reservation.

South County Housing Corporation (SCH): South County Housing Corporation is a nonprofit community development corporation. SCH was incorporated in 1979, as a nonprofit organization that develops affordable housing for low-income families, seniors, disabled adults, farm workers, and homeless persons. SCH provides services to Santa Clara, San Benito, Santa Cruz, and Monterey County in California. SCH has built 2,781 housing units, including 1,510 affordable apartments. SHC's model of combining mixed-income housing with on-site services addresses the unique needs of each, investing in the community's long-term success with recreational amenities, childcare facilities, and community buildings with computer labs. Working with strong community partners, SCH brings in services that enhance the lives of renters and homebuyers.

Southwest Housing Solutions: Southwest Housing Solutions began in 1979, and is a leader in the planning, development, and management of affordable housing and commercial property in southwest Detroit, Michigan. Its mission is to revitalize its community through collaborative, innovative, and high-quality projects, and by promoting homeownership. Southwest Housing Solutions provides housing to low- and moderate-income residents, including persons with mental illness and the homeless. Southwest Housing Solutions stimulates commercial and cultural development through mixed-use projects and also develops and implements neighborhood preservation initiatives.

The Community Builders, Inc. (TCB): TCB is the leading nonprofit developer of mixed-income housing in the United States. Its mission is to build and sustain strong communities where people of all incomes can achieve their full potential. TCB realizes its mission by developing, financing, and operating high-quality housing and implementing neighborhood self-help initiatives to drive economic opportunity for its residents. Since 1964, TCB has constructed or preserved over 320 affordable and mixed-income housing developments and secured over $2.5 billion in project financing from public and private sources. Today, TCB owns or manages more than 10,000 apartments in 14 states and Washington, DC. TCB is headquartered in Boston with regional hubs in Chicago and Washington, DC.

The Reinvestment Fund (TRF): TRF is a CDFI that manages over $700 million in capital and has made over $1.2 billion in community investments, financing over 2,750 projects since its inception in 1985. In pursuit of its mission, TRF finances community businesses using loan, equity, and other financing tools. TRF supports its financing with a strong research and policy analysis capacity that has become a highly regarded source of unbiased information for public officials and private investors. TRF's analytical strength is also reflected in its national online data and mapping tool that is available for all internet users at www.policymap.com. The tool offers thousands of data indicators to help users understand a place, compare places, or track investments in a place.

Volunteer of America National Services (VOANS): Volunteers of America National Services is a subsidiary of Volunteers of America, a national faith-based organization founded in 1896 that is dedicated to helping those in need through comprehensive programs including housing and healthcare. Volunteers of America helps more than 2.5 million people in over 400 communities in 46 states as well as the District of Columbia and Puerto Rico. The organization supports and empowers America's most vulnerable groups, including veterans, at-risk youth, the frail elderly, men and women returning from prison, homeless individuals and families, people with disabilities, and those recovering from addictions.

Western Community Housing, Inc. (WCH): WCH is a California nonprofit public benefit corporation that was founded in 1999 and is headquartered in Costa Mesa, California. WCH also maintains a regional office in Los Angeles, California. WCH's mission is to provide affordable housing and social service programs to very low-, low- and moderate-income families and seniors residing in affordable rental housing communities.

Women's Development Corporation (Wdc): Wdc a leader in the design, development, and production of housing for low-income families, the elderly and groups with special needs. In 1979, Wdc was founded by professional women with expertise in architecture and design, project and property management, community planning, historic preservation, and neighborhood development. Wdc staff consists of women and men dedicated to providing excellence in design and thoughtfulness in building, through which they strengthen communities and lives. Federal, state, and private financing allows Wdc to produce safe, desirable, and permanent housing for Rhode Island cities and towns. With these funds, Wdc preserves and restores historic buildings, constructs new, environmentally responsible housing, and revitalizes neighborhoods. Wdc also serves as an impetus for economic development by enhancing tax revenues for cities and towns and creating local construction and management jobs.

APPENDIX 2: ABBREVIATIONS & ACRONYMS

BEA	Bank Enterprise Award Program
CDE	Community Development Entity
CDFI	Community Development Financial Institutions
CDFI Fund	Community Development Financial Institutions Fund
CIIS	Community Investment Impact System
CMF	Capital Magnet Fund
FA	CDFI Program Financial Assistance Award
HERA	Housing and Economic Recovery Act of 2008
HFFI	Healthy Food Financing Initiative
ILR	Institution Level Report
LIHTC	Low Income Housing Tax Credit
NACA	Native American CDFI Assistance Program
NMTC	New Markets Tax Credit
SECA	CDFI Program Small and/or Emerging CDFI Financial Assistance
TLR	Transaction Level Report

APPENDIX 3: CAPITAL MAGNET FUND AWARDEE EXAMPLES OF WORK

The following project stories are examples of the work to date by Capital Magnet Fund awardees. The list does not include every project supported by Capital Magnet Fund awards, but rather were compiled from voluntary submissions by the Capital Magnet Fund awardees. The stories are listed alphabetically by state.

These stories are meant to illustrate the variety of projects and results from the Capital Magnet Fund program.

ALASKA

Volunteers of America National Services
Affordable Housing   40

SAN CARLOS APACHE RESERVATION (ARIZONA)

San Carlos Housing Authority
Affordable Housing   42

CALIFORNIA

Century Housing Corporation
Affordable Housing   44

Low Income Investment Fund
Senior Housing   46

South County Housing Corporation
Chronically Homeless Housing   48

Western Community Housing, Inc.
Affordable Housing (15 units set aside for homeless with a mental illness)   50

Western Community Housing, Inc.
Senior Housing   52

Western Community Housing, Inc.
Affordable Housing   54

COLORADO

Low Income Investment Fund
Health Center   56

DISTRICT OF COLUMBIA

The Reinvestment Fund, Inc.
Affordable Housing   58

HAWAII

Rural Community Assistance Corporation
Senior Housing   60

IDAHO

Northwest Real Estate Capital Corp.
Affordable Housing (Rehabilitation)   62

Northwest Real Estate Capital Corp.
Affordable Housing (Rehabilitation)   64

Northwest Real Estate Capital Corp.
Senior Housing (Rehabilitation)   66

Northwest Real Estate Capital Corp.
Affordable Housing (Rehabilitation)   68

ILLINOIS

Local Initiatives Support Corporation
Mixed-Use Housing   70

The Community Builders, Inc.
Mixed-Use Housing 72

LOUISIANA

Volunteers of America National Services
Veterans Housing 74

MARYLAND

The Reinvestment Fund, Inc.
Affordable Housing 76

MASSACHUSETTS

Massachusetts Housing Partnership
Affordable Housing 78

Massachusetts Housing Partnership
Affordable Housing 80

Massachusetts Housing Partnership
Affordable Housing 82

MICHIGAN

Great Lakes Capital Fund Nonprofit Housing Corporation
Affordable Housing (Rehabilitation) 84

Southwest Housing Solutions
Affordable Housing (Rehabilitation) 86

Southwest Housing Solutions
Wellness Center 88

Southwest Housing Solutions
Affordable Housing (Special Needs & Homeless)   90

Southwest Housing Solutions
Affordable Housing   92

Southwest Housing Solutions
Affordable Housing (Rehabilitation)   94

Volunteers of America National Services
Senior Housing   96

MISSISSIPPI

Hope Enterprise Corporation
Affordable Housing (Rehabilitation)   98

NEVADA

Idaho-Nevada Community Development Financial Institution
Senior Housing   100

Idaho-Nevada Community Development Financial Institution
Senior Housing   102

NEW HAMPSHIRE

New Hampshire Community Loan Fund, Inc.
Affordable Housing   104

OHIO

Ohio Capital Finance Corporation
Affordable Housing (Rehabilitation)   106

Ohio Capital Finance Corporation
Senior Housing 108

OREGON

Northwest Real Estate Capital Corp.
Affordable Housing (Rehabilitation) 110

PENNSYLVANIA

The Reinvestment Fund, Inc.
Mixed-Use Housing 112

RHODE ISLAND

Women's Development Corporation
Senior Housing 114

Women's Development Corporation
Affordable Housing 116

TEXAS

Low Income Investment Fund
Senior Housing 118

WISCONSIN

Forward Community Investments
Dental Facility 120

Great Lakes Capital Fund Nonprofit Housing Corporation
Affordable Housing for Disabled (Rehabilitation) 122

Trailside Heights Apartments

A CAPITAL MAGNET FUND PROJECT

VOLUNTEERS OF AMERICA NATIONAL SERVICES

Trailside Heights Apartments is a newly constructed, 66-unit townhome community for families in Anchorage, Alaska. This service-enriched housing features two- and three-bedroom homes and is located near many family-friendly amenities. An on-site community center offers a computer lab, meeting room, laundry facilities, and exercise equipment.

The project provides affordable housing to families and is restricted to households earning 50 percent to 60 percent of the area median income or less. For the first phase of this multi-phase planned community, the construction cost for Trailside Heights was $19.88 million. Financing included an award of Low Income Housing Tax Credits as well as a soft loan of $500,000 through the Capital Magnet Fund.

The Capital Magnet Fund program supports financing for the preservation, rehabilitation, or purchase of affordable housing for low-income communities and community service facilities such as day care centers, workforce development centers, and healthcare clinics. Projects financed using the Capital Magnet Funds have had a significant impact on reducing the lack of affordable housing in the communities in which they are located. Whether it be senior housing in Sheridan, Wyoming, family housing in Anchorage, Alaska, or permanent supportive

$5M
CAPITAL MAGNET FUND AWARD

"All of the projects we have financed using the Capital Magnet Funds have had a significant impact on reducing the lack of affordable housing in the communities in which they are located. Whether it be senior housing in Sheridan, Wyoming, family housing in Anchorage, Alaska or permanent supportive housing in Denver, Colorado, none of these very needed properties would have been developed or acquired without the Capital Magnet Fund award, ensuring long-term affordability for the residents of those communities."

Patrick Sheridan
Senior Vice President of Housing Development
Volunteers of America National Services

housing in Denver, Colorado, the Capital Magnet Fund award funds played an integral part in ensuring long-term affordability for the residents of those communities. With its CMF allocation, the Volunteers of America National Services is in the process of achieving the following impacts:

- Total award: $5 million
- Projects supported : 11
- Construction jobs created: 806
- Award leverage ratio: 1:13
- Leveraged $85,807,168 in total project costs
- Housing units completed: 215
- Housing units under development: 446

About Volunteer of America National Services (VOANS):
Volunteers of America National Services is a subsidiary of Volunteers of America, a national faith-based organization founded in 1896 that is dedicated to helping those in need through comprehensive programs including housing and health care. Volunteers of America helps more than 2.5 million people in over 400 communities in 46 states as well as the District of Columbia and Puerto Rico. The organization supports and empowers America's most vulnerable groups, including veterans, at-risk youth, the frail elderly, men and women returning from prison, homeless individuals and families, people with disabilities, and those recovering from addictions.

FOR MORE INFORMATION ABOUT THE IMPACT OF CDFIs ACROSS THE COUNTRY, VISIT WWW.CDFIFUND.GOV

ARIZONA

Housing & Renovation on Tribal Lands

A CAPITAL MAGNET FUND PROJECT

SAN CARLOS HOUSING AUTHORITY

The San Carlos Housing Authority, the tribally-designated housing entity of the San Carlos Apache Tribe, received a $1 million Capital Magnet Fund award that it has leveraged into almost $13 million with the Low Income Housing Tax Credit (LIHTC) program.

With the Capital Magnet Fund award, the San Carlos Housing Authority was able to build 31 new housing units and renovate 50 existing units, creating a lasting change for its community.

If the San Carlos Housing Authority did not have the Capital Magnet Fund award to bridge the financing gap, the projects would not have been possible because traditional borrowing and lending of money is virtually nonexistent on tribal trust land. The need for housing on the reservation is immense, but the ability to finance new homes with traditional methods is minimal.

$1M

CAPITAL MAGNET FUND AWARD

"With a combined scope that includes renovating 50 existing units and building 30 new homes, the San Carlos Homes V and San Carlos Homes VI projects themselves are substantial. But both projects have also ignited larger scale redevelopment initiatives in their respective communities. The San Carlos Homes V units represent just a small fraction of the homes that will be built in the Bylas District Master Plan, which will also include community areas and a new school. Additionally, San Carlos Homes VI has already prompted the development of additional units in the Tulapai Acres Subdivision. These projects have proved vital to our momentum for improving the way of life for our tribal members."

Ronald Boni
Executive Director
San Carlos Housing Authority

The San Carlos Housing Authority Leverage Debt Fund LLC made two loans with its Capital Magnet Fund award: San Carlos Homes V and San Carlos Homes VI. The first loan was for $459,308 to the San Carlos Homes V project, which was leveraged 14 times into $6,442,885 in equity from the LIHTC investor. The second loan of $401,458 went to San Carlos Homes VI, which was leveraged 16 times into $6,555,722 in investor equity. The remaining Capital Magnet Fund award will be used for any cost overruns on the projects as they are completed in the next few months.

In addition to housing, the San Carlos Housing Authority projects include three community buildings in these two developments that provide gathering and communal space for the projects' residents.

About San Carlos Housing Authority: The San Carlos Housing Authority (SCHA) is the tribal-designated housing entity of the San Carlos Apache Tribe in southeastern Arizona. The SCHA was established in 1961 and is the only provider of affordable housing on the San Carlos Reservation. The SCHA received the 2012 Most Valuable Partner Award from the U.S. Department of Housing and Urban Development for the 220 new homes that have been built within the San Carlos Apache Indian Reservation.

FOR MORE INFORMATION ABOUT THE IMPACT OF CDFIs ACROSS THE COUNTRY, VISIT WWW.CDFIFUND.GOV

CALIFORNIA

Affordable Housing in South Lake Tahoe

A CAPITAL MAGNET FUND PROJECT

CENTURY HOUSING CORPORATION

Century Housing Corporation (Century) used its own equity and other financial facilities to leverage its Capital Magnet Fund award to finance the creation and preservation of affordable housing throughout California. Century has used its initial Capital Magnet Fund award and is now reinvesting the funding into four additional projects. All of the projects are deeply affordable to tenants with incomes at or below 60 percent of the area median income.

One project that is presently in development is in South Lake Tahoe in Northern California and will create 48 affordable homes to low-income families in the area. (Pictured)

Another project is an existing affordable development that will rehabilitate 129 affordable units for low-income families in Colton, California, which was a city hit hard by the downturn in the economy. It was difficult for many lenders to consider financing a project in this area but fortunately Century, through the Capital Magnet Fund, was able to meet the needs of the nonprofit buyer.

$5M

CAPITAL MAGNET FUND AWARD

"Through the Capital Magnet Fund, Century has been able to increase our lending activity, which has resulted in the creation and preservation of 632 affordable homes for low-income families and seniors throughout California. Century will continue to use the funds to reinvest in our communities so seniors and families can have a dignified place to call home."

Aaron Wooler
Senior Vice President
Century Housing Corporation

About Century Housing Corporation: Century finances affordable housing developments throughout California. From bridge loans to acquisition loans to construction loans, Century has worked for more than 15 years to provide tax-credit developers and infill developers with innovative loans and responsive service. Century invests in homes and communities so that low-income individuals and families may have a dignified living environment, achieve economic independence, and enjoy healthful and vital places to live and work. Century believes that a just society provides safe, quality and affordable housing for all.

FOR MORE INFORMATION ABOUT THE IMPACT OF CDFIs ACROSS THE COUNTRY, VISIT WWW.CDFIFUND.GOV

CALIFORNIA

Eucalyptus Park

A CAPITAL MAGNET FUND PROJECT

LOW INCOME INVESTMENT FUND

The Low Income Investment Fund (LIIF) provided Thomas Safran and Associates (TSA), an established for-profit affordable housing developer, with a $12.5 million acquisition loan for the purchase of Eucalyptus Park Apartments in Inglewood, California.

LIIF was the lead lender in a three-party participation with Enterprise Community Loan Fund and the Calvert Foundation. LIIF used $782,000 of Capital Magnet Funds (CMFs) to provide a credit enhancement for its portion of the loan.

LIIF's support is enabling TSA to preserve 93 units of affordable apartments for seniors, all of which receive Section 8 rental assistance. With LIIF's financing, TSA will acquire and rehabilitate the existing buildings. In addition to the rehabilitation, TSA intends to extend the Section 8 housing assistance payments contract, currently on annual renewals, for 20 years in order to preserve the long-term affordability of the property.

Eucalyptus Park is located in close proximity to Inglewood's downtown district, giving residents ready access to public transportation and commercial services.

$6M

CAPITAL MAGNET FUND AWARD

The Low Income Investment Fund (LIIF) was awarded $6 million from the U.S. Department of the Treasury's Community Development Financial Institutions Fund's Capital Magnet Fund (CMF) program in 2010. The CMF program supports LIIF's efforts to finance the preservation, rehabilitation, and construction of affordable housing in low-income communities. LIIF seeks to deploy its CMF capital across its regions, which include California, the Pacific Northwest, the New York metropolitan area, the Northeast, the Washington, DC metropolitan area, Colorado, Texas, and Louisiana.

Nancy O. Andrews
President and CEO
Low Income Investment Fund

The CMF enables LIIF to provide flexible capital to high-capacity developers operating in challenging markets. Specifically, LIIF uses CMF capital to offer borrowers lower interest rates, flexible collateral arrangements, and higher loan-to-value ratios than would otherwise be possible. Without the funds available from LIIF through CMF, many developers would not have been able to successfully acquire, rehabilitate, and ultimately preserve affordable housing properties in competitive markets.

The CMF funds have allowed LIIF to partner and share risk with these developers, allowing the developers to use their organizational equity across more projects and maximize the affordable housing units preserved and their impact in their target communities.

About the Low Income Investment Fund: As a leading national community development financial institution, LIIF invests capital in low-income people and communities. Since its founding in 1984, LIIF has invested $1.3 billion in projects serving highly distressed neighborhoods. Through its financing and technical assistance, LIIF has served 1.4 million people and generated $25 billion in family and societal benefits.

FOR MORE INFORMATION ABOUT THE IMPACT OF CDFIs ACROSS THE COUNTRY, VISIT WWW.CDFIFUND.GOV

CALIFORNIA

Gilroy Sobrato Apartments

A CAPITAL MAGNET FUND PROJECT

SOUTH COUNTY HOUSING CORPORATION

To date, the Capital Magnet Fund award has enabled South County Housing Corporation to provide gap financing for 76 completed apartments; 24 completed townhomes; 108 apartments under construction; and 30 self-help homes just starting construction. The rental projects are restricted to 60 percent of the area median income and the for-sale homes are restricted to 80 percent of the area median income and below.

One project is the Gilroy Sobrato Apartments, a 26-studio apartment building of permanent housing for the chronically homeless. The apartment amenities include basketball and bocce ball courts, lawn space, gardens, laundry, a community room, and conference rooms for residents to meet with their caseworkers and social service providers.

Each resident receives a full spectrum of physical health, mental health, addiction recovery, and job training/ search services.

$1M

CAPITAL MAGNET FUND AWARD

"In the current environment of shrinking state and local funding, access to Capital Magnet Funds has provided critical, hard to obtain predevelopment financing that has allowed South County Housing to move projects forward. Without the award, we would not have had the ability to provide housing for hundreds of deserving families, individuals, and seniors."

Andy Lief
Director of Housing Development
South County Housing Corporation

About South County Housing Corporation (SCH): South County Housing is a nonprofit community development corporation. SCH was incorporated in 1979, as a nonprofit organization that develops affordable housing for low-income families, seniors, disabled adults, farm workers, and homeless persons. SCH provides services to Santa Clara, San Benito, Santa Cruz, and Monterey County in California. SCH has built 2,781 housing units, including 1,510 affordable apartments. SHC's model of combining mixed-income housing with on-site services addresses the unique needs of each project. SCH invests in the community's long-term success with recreational amenities, childcare facilities, and community buildings with computer labs. Working with strong community partners, SCH brings in services that enhance the lives of renters and homebuyers.

FOR MORE INFORMATION ABOUT THE IMPACT OF CDFIs ACROSS THE COUNTRY, VISIT WWW.CDFIFUND.GOV

CALIFORNIA

Cedar Glen Apartments

A CAPITAL MAGNET FUND PROJECT

WESTERN COMMUNITY HOUSING, INC.

Cedar Glen Apartments is a newly constructed 51-unit, 100 percent affordable family rental project with "special needs," targeted to low-income large families and clients who are in need of mental health supportive services, located in Riverside, California adjacent to the County's Department of Mental Health.

Western Community Housing made a Capital Magnet Fund (CMF) loan early on in the project's development timeline to cover predevelopment costs to the project prior to construction.

Unique to this large family project, almost half of the units are three- and four-bedroom units. The project's affordability ranges from 30 to 60 percent of the area median income with 15 units set aside targeting homeless persons with a mental illness.

The CMF loan assisted this project in funding up-front, predevelopment costs in a high-housing need area with a high foreclosure rate. When traditional lenders were hesitant to lend in this area and to a special needs project, the CMF loan fulfilled its mission by placing funds in this distressed area, hence providing economic growth and stimulus to this neighborhood community of Riverside.

$5M

CAPITAL MAGNET FUND AWARD

"Especially for projects that traditional financing was not available, and city funding was not permitted to purchase the land, our Capital Magnet Fund (CMF) loans allowed a stalled pipeline of Low Income Housing Tax Credit projects to be built for very deserving residents in needed neighborhoods."

Graham Espley-Jones
President
Western Community Housing, Inc.

About Western Community Housing, Inc. (WCH): WCH is a California nonprofit public benefit corporation that was founded in 1999 and is headquartered in Costa Mesa, California. WCH also maintains a regional office in Los Angeles, California. WCH's mission is to provide affordable housing and social service programs to very low-, low- and moderate income families and seniors residing in affordable rental housing communities.

FOR MORE INFORMATION ABOUT THE IMPACT OF CDFIs ACROSS THE COUNTRY, VISIT WWW.CDFIFUND.GOV

CALIFORNIA

Tavarua Senior Apartments

A CAPITAL MAGNET FUND PROJECT

WESTERN COMMUNITY HOUSING, INC.

Tavarua Senior Apartments is a newly constructed 50-unit, 100 percent affordable senior rental project located in Carlsbad, California. The project was planned on a redevelopment site that was an underutilized, foreclosed assisted living facility that degraded the neighborhood, but was ideally located across from a vibrant senior citizen center.

Western Community Housing made a Capital Magnet Fund (CMF) loan to cover predevelopment costs and bridge a financing gap during construction of the project.

The previous building was raised to make way for the new project that revitalized the neighborhood with a Mediterranean style three-story, elevator served senior community comprised of 40 one-bedroom units and 10 two-bedrooms units with a large community room for services. There are 10 units reserved for seniors with a mental illness.

This CMF loan allowed an infill foreclosed property to be developed into a quality living environment for low-income seniors, highlighting one of CMF's goals in helping move affordable housing projects through the development pipeline to completion.

$5M
CAPITAL MAGNET FUND AWARD

About Western Community Housing, Inc. (WCH): WCH is a California nonprofit public benefit corporation that was founded in 1999 and is headquartered in Costa Mesa, California. WCH also maintains a regional office in Los Angeles, California. WCH's mission is to provide affordable housing and social service programs to very low-, low- and moderate-income families and seniors residing in affordable rental housing communities.

FOR MORE INFORMATION
ABOUT THE IMPACT OF CDFIs
ACROSS THE COUNTRY,
VISIT WWW.CDFIFUND.GOV

The Grove at Sunset Court

A CAPITAL MAGNET FUND PROJECT

WESTERN COMMUNITY HOUSING, INC.

The Grove at Sunset Court is a newly constructed 54-unit, 100 percent affordable family rental project with a central community clubhouse, located in the Brentwood Boulevard Redevelopment Area within Brentwood, California.

Western Community Housing made a Capital Magnet Fund (CMF) loan to the project to cover land and predevelopment costs to keep the project progressing toward the construction start deadline stipulated in the state agency regulations.

The project revitalized a corner on a major residential and commercial corridor that serves as the gateway into downtown and offered 75 percent of the units at a deeply affordable area median income between 30 to 50 percent for the benefit of very low-income families.

The CMF loan successfully allowed the project to meet its start of construction and completion deadlines and deliver this affordable family community to low-income residents in a high housing need and distressed area of Brentwood.

CAPITAL MAGNET FUND AWARD

"It has been a real struggle over the last several years to put together adequate financing for low income housing tax credit projects, but CMF has helped tremendously with predevelopment loans and bridge loans through our low-interest rate CMF loan program."

Graham Espley-Jones
President
Western Community Housing, Inc.

About Western Community Housing, Inc. (WCH): WCH is a California nonprofit public benefit corporation that was founded in 1999 and is headquartered in Costa Mesa, California. WCH also maintains a regional office in Los Angeles, California. WCH's mission is to provide affordable housing and social service programs to very low-, low- and moderate-income families and seniors residing in affordable rental housing communities.

FOR MORE INFORMATION ABOUT THE IMPACT OF CDFIs ACROSS THE COUNTRY, VISIT WWW.CDFIFUND.GOV

COLORADO

West End Health Center

A CAPITAL MAGNET FUND PROJECT

LOW INCOME INVESTMENT FUND

The Low Income Investment Fund (LIIF) provided the Colorado Coalition for the Homeless (CCH), a leading developer and manager of mixed use-supportive housing and service facilities in Colorado, with a $500,000 tenant improvement loan for the West End Health Center in Denver.

The West End Health Center, a 7,400 square-foot facility co-located with a 101-unit mixed-used affordable housing development, provides a host of services including primary health care, mental health care, substance treatment counseling, pharmacy and nursing services, and patient education. The clinic is projected to employ eight full-time employees and serve 1,200 Medicaid-qualified clients in its first year.

The 100 percent affordable housing development, financed separately, includes 50 supportive housing units for homeless individuals and families. The new clinic will cater to the 50 supportive units, as well as families in the surrounding community. LIIF's financing, which included a $58,000 credit enhancement from the Capital Magnet Fund, helped CCH complete the build out of the health clinic.

$6M

CAPITAL MAGNET FUND AWARD

The Capital Magnet Fund's ability to absorb risk and provide favorable terms has supported LIIF's growth into new geographies, infusing more community development capital into markets. To date, LIIF has used CMF capital to credit enhance projects in Houston, Texas and Denver, Colorado, two new markets for the organization.

Nancy O. Andrews
President and CEO
Low Income Investment Fund

The CMF enables LIIF to provide flexible capital to high-capacity developers operating in challenging markets. Specifically, LIIF uses CMF capital to offer borrowers lower-interest rates, flexible collateral arrangements and higher loan-to-value ratios than would otherwise be possible. Its terms enable LIIF to fill gaps in high-impact projects that have resulted in more economic development activity in underserved communities. With the CMF, LIIF was able to support developers in today's difficult funding environment. The CMF enhanced LIIF's ability to provide financing that responded to the needs of the market.

About the Low Income Investment Fund: As a leading national community development financial institution, LIIF invests capital in low-income people and communities. Since its founding in 1984, LIIF has invested $1.3 billion in projects serving highly distressed neighborhoods. Through its financing and technical assistance, LIIF has served 1.4 million people and generated $25 billion in family and societal benefits.

FOR MORE INFORMATION ABOUT THE IMPACT OF CDFIs ACROSS THE COUNTRY, VISIT WWW.CDFIFUND.GOV

DISTRICT OF COLUMBIA

Anacostia Condominiums

A CAPITAL MAGNET FUND PROJECT

THE REINVESTMENT FUND

Located in the Anacostia neighborhood of Southeast Washington DC, this project is rehabbing and reconfiguring six attached apartment buildings that have been vacant for close to a decade.

The development will create 24 two-bedroom condominium units. The for-sale units will be affordable to households earning between 50 percent to 80 percent of the area median income.

While the units are restricted to families earning 80 percent of the area median income, the prices allow households earning just 22 percent of the area median income and 31 percent of the area median income, respectively, to buy. This provides an extremely broad buyer pool as compared to many projects that have a far smaller eligibility window.

The project is a few blocks from the District's Department of Housing and Community Development's (DHCD) new headquarters building at Good Hope Road and MLK Boulevard.

The new DHCD building is part of a larger economic development effort that has brought new employment, new retail, and better foot traffic to the neighborhood.

$5M

CAPITAL MAGNET FUND AWARD

"The Capital Magnet Fund is an important source of flexible and predictable seed capital needed to support housing development in highly-distressed markets. The strongest indication of its impact can be seen in the Anacostia Condominium project in Washington, DC, as well as East Baltimore's Oliver neighborhood. Vacant homes in the Baltimore neighborhood have dropped by 64 percent since 2006, entirely because of the CMF-supported housing development."

Don Hinkle-Brown
President & CEO
The Reinvestment Fund

Also included in this effort is a new 22,000 square foot state-of-the-art public library at 1800 Good Hope Road, just two blocks from the project.

Also nearby are the Frederick Douglass Museum, Fort Stanton Park, and the Anacostia historic district that features a number of 19th century homes. The area is well served by buses that run along Good Hope and MLK Boulevard and that serve the Anacostia Metro station, about 12 blocks away.

About The Reinvestment Fund (TRF): TRF is a Community Development Financial Institution (CDFI) that manages over $700 million in capital and has made over $1.2 billion in community investments, financing over 2,750 projects since its inception in 1985. In pursuit of its mission, TRF finances community businesses using loan, equity, and other financing tools. TRF supports its financing with a strong research and policy analysis capacity that has become a highly regarded source of unbiased information for public officials and private investors. TRF's analytical strength is also reflected in its national online data and mapping tool that is available for all internet users at www.policymap.com. The tool offers thousands of data indicators to help users understand a place, compare places, or track investments in a place.

FOR MORE INFORMATION ABOUT THE IMPACT OF CDFIs ACROSS THE COUNTRY, VISIT WWW.CDFIFUND.GOV

Mohouli Senior Housing Project

A CAPITAL MAGNET FUND PROJECT

RURAL COMMUNITY ASSISTANCE CORPORATION

Statistics concerning the graying of America are startling — according to the Administration on Aging, the older population, persons 65 years or older, numbered 39.6 million in 2009 (the latest year for which data is available). They represented 12.9 percent of the U.S. population, about one in every eight Americans. By 2030, there will be about 72.1 million older persons, more than twice their number in 2000.

Perhaps nowhere in Hawaii is this trend more evident than in Hilo where 39 percent of the island's seniors currently reside. Overwhelmingly, these seniors tend to have incomes far below the area median income and subsequently struggle to pay for even the most basic of needs. In fact, the area is home to nearly 4,000 single and two-person senior households with incomes of less than $25,000.

As housing prices in Hawaii continue to escalate, the need for affordable senior housing has spiraled, with scores of older island residents currently on waiting lists for the 218 affordable senior housing units available in the South Hilo area.

With its Capital Magnet Fund award, the Rural Community Assistance Corporation (RCAC) made a $4 million loan for construction of a 60-unit low-income senior housing project

$2M
CAPITAL MAGNET FUND AWARD

"Capital Magnet Funding allowed RCAC to be the primary private construction lender for a project that provided 60 units of badly needed very low-income senior housing in Hilo Hawaii. This will be the first of many uses of the CMF fund as we revolve and leverage the grant in the future."

Michael Carroll
Loan Fund Director
Rural Community Assistance Corporation

in Hilo, Hawaii. The Capital Magnet Fund award allowed RCAC to make a loan twice the size of its normal loan limit and to reduce the interest rate by .5 percent enabling RCAC to be the primary private construction lender, leveraging public sources and equity.

The Need: RCAC held a lottery for the units on May 30, 2013. At that time there were 248 persons interested in the 60-unit project and there has been more interest since then. There are currently hundreds on the wait list.

About Rural Community Assistance Corporation (RCAC): RCAC is a nonprofit organization that provides technical assistance, training, and financing so rural communities achieve their goals and visions. Headquartered in West Sacramento, California, RCAC's employees serve rural communities in 13 western states, plus the western Pacific. RCAC's work encompasses a wide range of services including technical assistance and training for environmental infrastructure. affordable housing development. economic and leadership development. and community development finance. These services are available to a variety of communities and organizations including communities with populations of fewer than 50,000, other nonprofit groups. and tribal organizations.

FOR MORE INFORMATION ABOUT THE IMPACT OF CDFIs ACROSS THE COUNTRY, VISIT WWW.CDFIFUND.GOV

IDAHO

Windwood Apartments

A CAPITAL MAGNET FUND PROJECT

NORTHWEST REAL ESTATE CAPITAL CORP.

Windwood Apartments is located in Jerome, the county seat and largest city in Jerome County, Idaho. Jerome is a small-scale community with an established older downtown core. The property's surrounding neighborhood consists of older single family homes with a limited number of apartment complexes. The neighborhood was primarily built out in the 1950s through the 1980s.

Northwest Real Estate Capital Corp. (NWRECC) has managed Windwood Apartments since December 2000 and acquired it in May 2010. The acquisition and moderate rehabilitation of this 30-unit HUD subsidized family property utilized a competitive 9 percent Low Income Housing Tax Credit purchased by Homestead Capital, a wholly owned subsidiary of the National Equity Fund (NEF), tax credit equity bridge financing, construction financing, and permanent financing by the Utah Community Reinvestment Corporation (UCRC) as a lender.

The three two-story townhouse style and one single-story buildings were in fair condition. There are six one-bedroom, 18 two-bedroom and six three-bedroom units serving Jerome's family population. The common area includes a community building with laundry facilities, children's play area, and a new outdoor picnic shelter. The moderate rehabilitation focused on

$500K

CAPITAL MAGNET FUND AWARD

improving the exterior structural conditions such as roof, siding, window and sliding door replacement, parking lot, sidewalk, and fencing repair and replacement. Interior structural conditions were improved by replacing kitchen and bathroom cabinets and countertops, along with floor covering replacement and fixture and appliance replacement as needed. Additionally, the rehabilitation brought common areas and the two accessible units up to current ADA requirements.

About Northwest Real Estate Capital Corp.: Northwest Real Estate Capital Corp. was formed in 1999. It is a regional tax-exempt affordable housing preservation company headquartered in Boise, Idaho. Since inception, the company has acquired, financed, rehabilitated, preserved, and manages over $130 million of new and existing multi-family housing in the Northwest, benefiting low-income families, the elderly, and disabled persons with incomes below 40 percent of the adjusted median income. The company's preservation activities include most types of federally regulated housing, including HUD Section 8, 202, 236, 811, Home, Section 42, USDA Section 515, and related affordable housing programs.

FOR MORE INFORMATION
ABOUT THE IMPACT OF CDFIs
ACROSS THE COUNTRY,
VISIT **WWW.CDFIFUND.GOV**

IDAHO

Pioneer Square Apartments

A CAPITAL MAGNET FUND PROJECT

NORTHWEST REAL ESTATE CAPITAL CORP.

Pioneer Square Apartments is located in Boise, Idaho, within the downtown core of the city. The core is nearly at full build-out, with very few vacant sites remaining. Nearby properties include a mix of office, high rise, retail, hotels, and special use properties. The downtown core is Boise's cultural center and home to many small businesses, with an array of shopping and dining choices. Overall, the neighborhood has an above average appeal for an apartment complex.

The acquisition and moderate rehabilitation allowed for the continuing use of 43-units of HUD subsidized family property. The project was financed utilizing competitive Low Income Housing Tax Credits purchased by PNC Real Estate, tax credit equity bridge financing, construction financing, soft sponsor financing, and permanent financing with PNC Real Estate as lender.

The rehabilitation began in 2011 and was completed in eight months. The $1,790,252 in hard costs will preserve the useful life of Pioneer Square for the next 30+ years. Rehabilitation included new siding for all buildings. The siding included new thin brick façade on the lower portion of buildings, with hardiplank and metal above. Existing windows and sliding doors were replaced with new low-e vinyl windows and sliding

$500K

CAPITAL MAGNET FUND AWARD

"Our preservation of existing low-income housing is largely a rural community endeavor. In many instances our renovation of the local low-income apartment complex is the first new substantial investment in housing the community has seen for some time, so it generates a lot of local support and appreciation from the community, particularly the police, schools, and local government officials."

Brad A. Elg
President
Northwest Real Estate Capital Corp.

doors; new railings were added onto the second floor balconies; sections of iron fencing with brick pilasters added at strategic spots along the Pioneer Walkway. Most apartment patios facing the common pathways of the Pioneer Corridor were rebuilt with low brick partitions for privacy and appearance. Other exterior rehabilitation consisted of replacing roof and gutters; replacement or repair, sealcoat, and striping of asphalt pavement; repair of patios not facing the main roads/walkways; replacement of playground equipment and surface; some landscaping; all common areas and walkways were repaired as necessary and appropriate areas were improved to enhance accessibility.

Unit interiors rehabilitation included the replacement of all kitchen and bathroom cabinets and countertops; most carpets and all vinyl sheeting; kitchen appliances and fixtures were replaced as needed and the physically accessible unit was improved to meet current code requirements and an audio/visual accessible unit was added; through-the-wall air conditioning units were added in the master bedrooms.

About Northwest Real Estate Capital Corp.: Northwest Real Estate Capital Corp. was formed in 1999. It is a regional tax-exempt affordable housing preservation company headquartered in Boise, Idaho. Since inception, the company has acquired, financed, rehabilitated, preserved, and manages over $130 million of new and existing multi-family housing in the Northwest, benefiting low-income families, the elderly, and disabled persons with incomes below 40 percent of the adjusted median income. The company's preservation activities include most types of federally regulated housing, including HUD Section 8, 202, 236, 811, Home, Section 42, USDA Section 515, and related affordable housing programs.

FOR MORE INFORMATION ABOUT THE IMPACT OF CDFIs ACROSS THE COUNTRY, VISIT WWW.CDFIFUND.GOV

IDAHO

Mill Creek Apartments

A CAPITAL MAGNET FUND PROJECT

NORTHWEST REAL ESTATE CAPITAL CORP.

Mill Creek Apartments is located in Lewiston, Idaho in a mature, mixed-use neighborhood within five blocks of the Lewiston Central Business District. The business district consists primarily of offices, service businesses, and boutique shopping. The areas peripheral to Mill Creek Apartments are comprised of single and multi-family residences, offices, and commercial buildings housing primarily service businesses.

The three-story, two-winged building with a flat roof was in average condition for its age, but needed some moderate rehabilitation. There are 40 one-bedroom units serving Lewiston's elderly population, and a two-bedroom manager's unit. The common area includes an elevator, lobbies on each floor, accessible men's and women's separate rest rooms, recreation room with full kitchen and outdoor patio, laundry room, and a reading room/library.

The moderate rehabilitation focused on improving exterior structural conditions such as a roof, siding, windows, and sliding doors replacement, parking lot, sidewalk, and fence repair and/or replacement. Interior structural conditions were improved by replacing plumbing, kitchen and bathroom cabinets and countertops, along with vinyl and carpet floor covering

$500K

CAPITAL MAGNET FUND AWARD

"Our preservation of existing low-income housing is largely a rural community endeavor. In many instances our renovation of the local low-income apartment complex is the first new substantial investment in housing the community has seen for some time, so it generates a lot of local support and appreciation from the community, particularly the police, schools, and local government officials."

Brad A. Elg
President
Northwest Real Estate Capital Corp.

replacement and some fixture and appliance replacement as needed. Additionally, the rehabilitation brought the common areas and the four accessible units up to current ADA requirements. A new fire alarm system was also added.

About Northwest Real Estate Capital Corp.: Northwest Real Estate Capital Corp. was formed in 1999. It is a regional tax-exempt affordable housing preservation company headquartered in Boise, Idaho. Since inception, the company has acquired, financed, rehabilitated, preserved, and manages over $130 million of new and existing multi-family housing in the Northwest, benefiting low-income families, the elderly, and disabled persons with incomes below 40 percent of the adjusted median income. The company's preservation activities include most types of federally regulated housing, including HUD Section 8, 202, 236, 811, Home, Section 42, USDA Section 515, and related affordable housing programs.

FOR MORE INFORMATION ABOUT THE IMPACT OF CDFIs ACROSS THE COUNTRY, VISIT WWW.CDFIFUND.GOV

IDAHO

Coeur d'Alene Manor Apartments

A CAPITAL MAGNET FUND PROJECT

NORTHWEST REAL ESTATE CAPITAL CORP.

Coeur d'Alene Manor Apartments is located in Coeur d' Alene, Idaho. Coeur d' Alene is the largest city in Northern Idaho, and is part of the second largest metropolitan area in the state. Historically, the local economy was supported by timber, mining, and agriculture. However, in the recent years tourism has become the dominant industry. The city is located on the north shore of Lake Coeur d' Alene, a popular summer destination.

The area has received positive media attention in recent years, including being named by U.S. News and World Report as one of the 10 best cities in America to live. All of these factors have contributed to Coeur d' Alene being one of Idaho's fastest growing cities over the past decade. Demand for real estate near Coeur d' Alene has been so strong that two high-rise condominiums were developed in the 2000s.

Northwest Real Estate Capital Corp. (NWRECC), a Capital Magnet Fund awardee, purchased Coeur d'Alene Manor Apartments in May 2013. The apartments consist of five buildings (two stories each) and a single-story common area that features a leasing office, lounge room, kitchen, restroom, and attached laundry. The Coeur d'Alene Manor Apartments needs rehabilitation. Site work includes sidewalk repair and/or replacement, additional site lighting, new benches to the interior

$500K

CAPITAL MAGNET FUND AWARD

"Our preservation of existing low-income housing is largely a rural community endeavor. In many instances our renovation of the local low-income apartment complex is the first new substantial investment in housing the community has seen for some time, so it generates a lot of local support and appreciation from the community, particularly the police, schools, and local government officials."

Brad A. Elg
President
Northwest Real Estate Capital Corp.

courts, new bike rack to the central courtyard area, all new vinyl windows, new metal doors at unit entries, new roofing and underlayment, new fascia, patch and repair soffit material as necessary, and additional insulation to the attic. In addition, the siding will receive a new acrylic stucco finish over the existing Marblecrete on the exterior walls, and new guardrails to the stairs.

Apartment improvements include replacement of most ranges and range hoods and refrigerators (these will be replaced with energy star rated appliances), and all new kitchen cabinets and countertops. In the bathrooms, the existing tub and surrounds will be replaced, toilets, sinks, and faucets will be replaced as necessary, as well as all new bath vanities and flooring. All bedrooms will receive new battery operated smoke alarms and all hardwired smoke detectors will meet local regulations. One smoke detector will be a combination smoke/CO detector in each unit. Water heaters will be replaced as necessary.

Three of the units will be targeted to accessible modifications. One unit will also be a specialized unit for audio/visually-impaired residents.

About Northwest Real Estate Capital Corp.: Northwest Real Estate Capital Corp. was formed in 1999. It is a regional tax-exempt affordable housing preservation company headquartered in Boise, Idaho. Since inception, the company has acquired, financed, rehabilitated, preserved, and manages over $130 million of new and existing multi-family housing in the Northwest, benefiting low-income families, the elderly, and disabled persons with incomes below 40 percent of the adjusted median income. The company's preservation activities include most types of federally regulated housing, including HUD Section 8, 202, 236, 811, Home, Section 42, USDA Section 515, and related affordable housing programs.

FOR MORE INFORMATION
ABOUT THE IMPACT OF CDFIs
ACROSS THE COUNTRY,
VISIT WWW.CDFIFUND.GOV

Zapata Apartments

A CAPITAL MAGNET FUND PROJECT

LOCAL INITIATIVES SUPPORT CORPORATION

Bickerdike Redevelopment Corporation (BRC) is an experienced developer, property manager, and construction contractor that has been active in the Humboldt Park neighborhood of Chicago since 1967. Local Initiatives Support Corporation (LISC) was an early and steady supporter of BRC's activities; it has provided more than $2.6 million in grant support, $7.7 million in loan support, and $50 million in Low Income Housing Tax Credit investments through its affiliate, The National Equity Fund.

LISC's most recent support to BRC was for Zapata Apartments, a $25 million, 61-unit, four building mixed-use development in Chicago, Illinois. It provided a $1 million loan for BRC's acquisition of a number of the vacant lots, as well as predevelopment expenses while BRC assembled the public and private financing necessary for the project. Then, due to a change in City funding sources, Bickerdike turned to LISC to provide an additional $3.6 million bridge loan to advance proceeds from tax increment financing during construction. LISC was able to use $722,593 of its Capital Magnet Fund award toward the funding of the last and largest loan to this project.

The homes will be affordable to families earning less than 50 percent of area median Income and four units will be equipped for the hearing impaired. The development will also incorporate

CAPITAL MAGNET FUND AWARD

"The projects supported by our Capital Magnet Fund award provide tangible benefits to low-and moderate-income households and contribute to the revitalization of the surrounding neighborhoods."

Tiffany Sims
Credit Officer
LISC

many green elements including Energy Star appliances, energy efficient windows and heating/cooling systems. LISC received a $5 million award from the Capital Magnet Fund program of the CDFI Fund. The award, combined with funds from Morgan Stanley, was used to create the $23.75 million Neighborhood Revitalization Loan Fund focused on supporting affordable rental housing development. The following information highlights the overall impact LISC has been able to make with its allocation.

- Created/preserved 526 affordable affordable homes and apartments.

- Created approximately 74,000 square feet of space for supportive services and educational programs.

- Supported seven projects to date.

- Leveraged $138.4 million of total project costs.

About Local Initiatives Support Corporation (LISC): LISC is dedicated to helping community residents transform distressed neighborhoods into healthy and sustainable communities of choice and opportunity — good places to work, do business, and raise children. For over three decades, LISC has connected local organizations and community leaders with resources to revitalize neighborhoods and improve quality of life. The LISC model assembles private and public resources and directs it to locally-defined priorities. Its unique structure enables local organizations to access national resources and expertise and funding partners to leverage their investment and achieve an impact that is truly remarkable. LISC is a national organization with a community focus. LISC program staff work in 31 local offices and in many rural communities across the country. In collaboration with local community development groups, LISC staff help identify priorities and challenges, delivering the most appropriate support to meet local needs.

FOR MORE INFORMATION ABOUT THE IMPACT OF CDFIs ACROSS THE COUNTRY, VISIT WWW.CDFIFUND.GOV

ILLINOIS

Shops and Lofts at 47

A CAPITAL MAGNET FUND PROJECT

THE COMMUNITY BUILDERS, INC.

Heralded as a harbinger of better days to come, Shops and Lofts at 47 is a long awaited mixed-use development in Chicago's historic Bronzeville neighborhood slated for completion in 2014.

The $46.5 million complex is the first commercial and residential development in the area in more than 50 years. It will house 96 mixed-income rental apartments developed and managed by The Community Builders, Inc. (TCB), along with a total of 55,000 square feet of commercial space, developed by Skilken and TROY.

Capital Magnet Funds (CMFs) were used to fill a financial gap that threatened a complex financial closing. The commercial and residential spaces were split financially through the use of a condominium structure. This allowed for more diverse sources of funding, but also required that both the residential and commercial portions of the building had to close at the same time in order for the project to move forward. A grant to fund energy saving features in the residential portion of the project was not going to be provided until after the project closed. This posed a significant problem for investors and threatened to delay a project that would provide high-quality affordable housing and bring healthy foods to a community that otherwise lacked access. TCB was able to use $282,000 of its Capital

CAPITAL MAGNET FUND AWARD

"The Community Builders has a long history of revitalizing low-income communities. The ability to continue this work was strained by the market crisis in 2008 and 2009. The $5 million of Capital Magnet Funds allowed TCB to close transactions that were otherwise perceived as too risky by investors, provide bridge funding for slower financing, and allow for more flexibility in identifying other financial participants. By utilizing CMF funds, we were able to mitigate that risk and deliver projects on time to low-income communities."

Thomas Buonopane
Director of Finance
The Community Builders, Inc.

Magnet Fund award in the form of a guarantee to bridge the Illinois Department of Commerce and Economic Opportunity (DCEO) grant that would be secured after closing. TCB was confident the grant would be funded and determined the use of CMF funds carried limited risk and would ultimately be returned and reinvested in another project.

The use of CMF funds allowed for the successful development of this long underused corner that represents a new phase in the storied and proud history of the Bronzeville neighborhood. Previously a thriving community of largely black-owned businesses, civic life, and thought, Bronzeville was a cultural mecca in Chicago. But over the past several decades, Bronzeville suffered a trajectory of economic decline.

Shops and Lofts at 47 creates a foundation for jobs, housing, and commerce. A Walmart Neighborhood Market will be the anchor commercial tenant with a 41,000 square-foot store that will provide residents of the neighborhood with greater access to jobs and fresh food—both longstanding issues in the traditionally underserved community.

About The Community Builders, Inc. (TCB): TCB is the leading nonprofit developer of mixed-income housing in the United States. Its mission is to build and sustain strong communities where people of all incomes can achieve their full potential. TCB realizes its mission by developing, financing, and operating high-quality housing and implementing neighborhood self-help initiatives to drive economic opportunity for residents. Since 1964, TCB has constructed or preserved over 320 affordable and mixed-income housing developments and secured over $2.5 billion in project financing from public and private sources. Today, TCB owns or manages more than 10,000 apartments in 14 states and Washington, DC. TCB is headquartered in Boston with regional hubs in Chicago and Washington, DC.

FOR MORE INFORMATION
ABOUT THE IMPACT OF CDFIs
ACROSS THE COUNTRY,
VISIT **WWW.CDFIFUND.GOV**

LOUISIANA

Affordable Housing for Veterans

A CAPITAL MAGNET FUND PROJECT

VOLUNTEERS OF AMERICA NATIONAL SERVICES

Volunteers of America National Services has committed Capital Magnet Fund monies for the acquisition of an existing 41-unit garden style property without rent or income restrictions in Shreveport, Louisiana.

The property will be repurposed as a mixed-income property with at least 20 units set aside to serve veterans with HUD's Veterans Affairs Supportive Housing Program (VASH) vouchers and/or other housing subsidies.

After acquisition, all units will be restricted to the affordable housing limits of the Capital Magnet Fund award except for the VASH requirements.

Projects financed using the Capital Magnet Funds have had a significant impact on reducing the lack of affordable housing in the communities in which they are located.

With its CMF allocation, the Volunteers of America National Services is in the process of achieving the following impacts:

- Projects supported : 11
- Leveraged $85,807,168 in total project costs
- Housing units completed: 215
- Housing units under development: 446

CAPITAL MAGNET FUND AWARD

"All of the projects we have financed using the Capital Magnet Funds have had a significant impact on reducing the lack of affordable housing in the communities in which they are located. Whether it be senior housing in Sheridan, Wyoming, family housing in Anchorage, Alaska or permanent supportive housing in Denver, Colorado, none of these very needed properties would have been developed or acquired, ensuring long-term affordability for the residents of those communities."

Patrick Sheridan
Senior Vice President of Housing Development
Volunteers of America National Services

About Volunteer of America National Services (VOANS):
Volunteers of America National Services is a subsidiary of Volunteers of America, a national faith-based organization founded in 1896 that is dedicated to helping those in need through comprehensive programs including housing and healthcare. Volunteers of America helps more than 2.5 million people in over 400 communities in 46 states as well as the District of Columbia and Puerto Rico. The organization supports and empowers America's most vulnerable groups, including veterans, at-risk youth, the frail elderly, men and women returning from prison, homeless individuals and families, people with disabilities, and those recovering from addictions.

FOR MORE INFORMATION ABOUT THE IMPACT OF CDFIs ACROSS THE COUNTRY, VISIT WWW.CDFIFUND.GOV

MARYLAND

Preston Place

A CAPITAL MAGNET FUND PROJECT

THE REINVESTMENT FUND

Preston Place is a reinvestment effort in Baltimore's Oliver neighborhood and is adjacent to the Johns Hopkins Medical Campus and the East Baltimore Development Inc.'s $1.2 billion redevelopment effort. Preston Place is a complex of 150 new and rehabbed energy-efficient townhomes for rent and for-sale.

The project provides significant affordable housing and first-time homeownership opportunities to hardworking Baltimore families and initiates the rebirth of this neighborhood. The project is currently in its second phase of development. Total project costs for this phase was $7.16 million, $735,000 of which came through the Capital Magnet Fund award. The units are affordable to families with incomes at 30 percent to 80 percent of area median income.

Preston Place is a project of TRF DP, a partnership between The Reinvestment Fund (TRF) and Baltimoreans United in Leadership Development (BUILD), a community organizing network focused on community economic development, leadership, and community empowerment. TRF partnered with BUILD in 2002 to develop a revitalization plan for the Oliver neighborhood in East Baltimore. TRF DP was created to implement that plan and to acquire and develop land and buildings for affordable housing in distressed areas within Baltimore. TRF DP has investors

CAPITAL MAGNET FUND AWARD

"The Capital Magnet Fund is an important source of flexible and predictable seed capital needed to support housing development in highly distressed markets. The strongest indication of its impact can be seen in East Baltimore's Oliver neighborhood. Vacant homes in the neighborhood have dropped by 64 percent since 2006, entirely because of the CMF-supported housing development."

Don Hinkle-Brown
President & CEO
The Reinvestment Fund

that include the Archdiocese of Baltimore, Annie E. Casey Foundation, Charlesmead Foundation, Jewish Funds for Justice, Johns Hopkins University, Rouse Company Foundation, M&T Bank, and T. Rowe Price Foundation.

According to Nielsen estimates, the median income for a family living in Oliver in 2009 ranged from $11,250 to $17,750, compared to the state median family income of $82,923. At the start of TRF DP's work, 40.8 percent of the properties were vacant in the Preston Place target area. Today, the area has only 61 vacant homes out of 416 homes (14.6 percent); this is a 64 percent drop in vacant homes since 2006.

About The Reinvestment Fund (TRF): TRF is a Community Development Financial Institution (CDFI) that manages over $700 million in capital and has made over $1.2 billion in community investments, financing over 2,750 projects since its inception in 1985. In pursuit of its mission, TRF finances community businesses using loan, equity, and other financing tools. TRF supports its financing with a strong research and policy analysis capacity that has become a highly regarded source of unbiased information for public officials and private investors. TRF's analytical strength is also reflected in its national online data and mapping tool that is available for all internet users at www.policymap.com. The tool offers thousands of data indicators to help users understand a place, compare places, or track investments in a place.

FOR MORE INFORMATION ABOUT THE IMPACT OF CDFIs ACROSS THE COUNTRY, VISIT WWW.CDFIFUND.GOV

MASSACHUSETTS

Saint Polycarp Phase II

A CAPITAL MAGNET FUND PROJECT

MASSACHUSETTS HOUSING PARTNERSHIP

The Massachusetts Housing Partnership (MHP) uses lines of credit from the banking industry in combination with its Capital Magnet Fund (CMF) award to provide low-cost, fixed-rate long-term financing for affordable rental housing. MHP uses its CMF award to fund loan loss reserves and/or cash collateral to its funding banks. For Saint Polycarp II, MHP provided a $1.6 million first mortgage and over $94,000 in CMF funds to help the nonprofit Somerville Community Corp. turn a former church site into 29 units of affordable rental housing. Situated next to Cambridge and Boston, Somerville has become a popular area for students and high-paid professionals, and this has made the housing very expensive.

The bottom line: When the Somerville Community Corp. started developing the former Saint Polycarp church site, they had Erika and Virgilio Garcia in mind. Both came from El Salvador to Somerville as children and attended local schools. They became close at Friday youth church group meetings and married after high school. Erika has worked at a local bank since she was a teenager while Virgilio works nights at Harvard University's

CAPITAL MAGNET FUND AWARD

"Capital Magnet Funds have allowed MHP to help meet an unprecedented demand for affordable housing in Massachusetts. We've been able to double our lending volume over the past three fiscal years thanks in large part to the increased capital that the CDFI Fund has provided, and the $4 million in funding is allowing MHP to provide permanent financing for nearly 1,600 units of affordable housing, showcasing the power of this leveraging model to make a positive impact in our communities."

Mark A. Curtiss
Managing Director
Massachusetts Housing Partnership

walk-in clinic so he can take care of their two children and pursue his nursing assistant's degree during the day. Getting a two-bedroom apartment for $1,170 a month (utilities included) has enabled them to remain close to their jobs, family, public transportation, and school. "Somerville is getting expensive," said Erika. "Someday, we would love to own a house. Living at Saint Polycarp is helping us save for that day."

About the Massachusetts Housing Partnership (MHP): The Massachusetts Housing Partnership is a statewide public nonprofit affordable housing organization that works in concert with the Governor and the state Department of Housing and Community Development to help increase the supply of affordable housing in Massachusetts. MHP was established in 1985 to increase the state's overall rate of housing production and find creative new solutions to address the need for affordable housing. In 1990, the state legislature took that premise to heart, becoming the first and only state in the nation to pass an interstate banking act that requires companies that acquire Massachusetts banks to make funds available to MHP for affordable housing. MHP's Community Housing Initiatives team works with communities, local housing groups, and nonprofit developers on local housing initiatives. Using its bank-funded loan pool, MHP provides long-term financing for the development and preservation of affordable rental housing. MHP also offers the SoftSecond Loan Program, a first-time homebuyers mortgage program for families of low and moderate incomes.

FOR MORE INFORMATION ABOUT THE IMPACT OF CDFIs ACROSS THE COUNTRY, VISIT WWW.CDFIFUND.GOV

MASSACHUSETTS

Sudbury Duplexes

A CAPITAL MAGNET FUND PROJECT

MASSACHUSETTS HOUSING PARTNERSHIP

The Massachusetts Housing Partnership (MHP) uses lines of credit from the banking industry in combination with its Capital Magnet Fund (CMF) award to provide low-cost, fixed-rate long-term financing for affordable rental housing. MHP uses its CMF award to fund loan loss reserves and/or cash collateral to its funding banks.

For the Sudbury Duplexes, MHP provided the developer early technical assistance to determine project feasibility and then provided a $1.1 million first mortgage and $756,000 in zero percent interest second mortgage financing through a program designed to increase the supply of affordable housing in high-cost suburban communities that have good schools and are near jobs. MHP also used $58,627 from its CMF award to help the Sudbury Housing Authority replace four aging homes with duplexes, build another duplex on a fifth site, and remodel a sixth home for 11 total units of affordable rental housing.

The bottom line: Sudbury Housing Authority Director Jo-Ann Howe looked at over 20 sites before determining that her best chance of developing more affordable housing was to build new units on housing authority land. When asked why she didn't give

$4M

CAPITAL MAGNET FUND AWARD

"Capital Magnet Funds have allowed MHP to help meet an unprecedented demand for affordable housing in Massachusetts. We've been able to double our lending volume over the past three fiscal years thanks in large part to the increased capital that the CDFI Fund has provided, and the $4 million in funding is allowing MHP to provide permanent financing for nearly 1,600 units of affordable housing, showcasing the power of this leveraging model to make a positive impact in our communities."

Mark A. Curtiss
Managing Director
Massachusetts Housing Partnership

jobs, family, public transportation, and school. "Somerville is getting expensive," said Erika. "Someday, we would love to own a house. Living at Saint Polycarp is helping us save for that day."

About the Massachusetts Housing Partnership (MHP): The Massachusetts Housing Partnership is a statewide public nonprofit affordable housing organization that works in concert with the Governor and the state Department of Housing and Community Development to help increase the supply of affordable housing in Massachusetts. MHP was established in 1985 to increase the state's overall rate of housing production and find creative new solutions to address the need for affordable housing. In 1990, the state legislature took that premise to heart, becoming the first and only state in the nation to pass an interstate banking act that requires companies that acquire Massachusetts banks to make funds available to MHP for affordable housing. MHP's Community Housing Initiatives team works with communities, local housing groups, and nonprofit developers on local housing initiatives. Using its bank-funded loan pool, MHP provides long-term financing for the development and preservation of affordable rental housing. MHP also offers the SoftSecond Loan Program, a first-time homebuyers mortgage program for families of low and moderate incomes.

FOR MORE INFORMATION ABOUT THE IMPACT OF CDFIs ACROSS THE COUNTRY, VISIT WWW.CDFIFUND.GOV

MASSACHUSETTS

Rice Silk Mill

A CAPITAL MAGNET FUND PROJECT

MASSACHUSETTS HOUSING PARTNERSHIP

Massachusetts Housing Partnership provided an $800,000 first mortgage and over $70,000 from its Capital Magnet Fund award to help Rees-Larkin Development turn an abandoned mill in a neighborhood hard-hit by foreclosures into 45 rental homes. Forty-three of the units are affordable and the project includes 19 two-bedroom and seven three-bedroom apartments for families.

The bottom line: Jobless in Florida, Cale Bassett found a job at a paper company in Pittsfield and moved his wife Cheryl and three young children into a market-rate, three-bedroom apartment at Rice Silk Mill in Pittsfield, an industrial town in the northwest corner of Massachusetts.

Cale and Cheryl say the $1,150 per month rent is a bit of a stretch on his $30,000 per year salary, but with utilities included, the family's costs are predictable. Their home is right next to an elementary school, making life possible with one car, which allows them to dream that they are on their way to making a good home in Massachusetts.

$4M

CAPITAL MAGNET FUND AWARD

"The Massachusetts Housing Partnership (MHP) uses lines of credit from the banking industry in combination with Capital Magnet Funds to provide low-cost, fixed-rate long-term financing for affordable rental housing. MHP uses its Capital Magnet Fund award to fund loan loss reserves and/or cash collateral to its funding banks."

Mark A. Curtiss
Managing Director
Massachusetts Housing Partnership

About the Massachusetts Housing Partnership (MHP): The Massachusetts Housing Partnership is a statewide public nonprofit affordable housing organization that works in concert with the Governor and the state Department of Housing and Community Development to help increase the supply of affordable housing in Massachusetts. MHP was established in 1985 to increase the state's overall rate of housing production and find creative new solutions to address the need for affordable housing. In 1990, the state legislature took that premise to heart, becoming the first and only state in the nation to pass an interstate banking act that requires companies that acquire Massachusetts banks to make funds available to MHP for affordable housing. MHP's Community Housing Initiatives team works with communities, local housing groups, and nonprofit developers on local housing initiatives. Using its bank-funded loan pool, MHP provides long-term financing for the development and preservation of affordable rental housing. MHP also offers the SoftSecond Loan Program, a first-time homebuyers mortgage program for families of low and moderate incomes.

FOR MORE INFORMATION ABOUT THE IMPACT OF CDFIs ACROSS THE COUNTRY, VISIT WWW.CDFIFUND.GOV

MICHIGAN

Pineshores Apartments

A CAPITAL MAGNET FUND PROJECT

GREAT LAKES CAPITAL FUND NONPROFIT HOUSING CORPORATION

In 2011, Pineshores Limited Dividend Housing Association Limited Partnership (Pineshores), a Michigan limited partnership, purchased and implemented a moderate rehabilitation of Pineshores Apartments in Flint, Michigan. The general partner of Pineshores is a limited liability company controlled by Rodney M. Lockwood, Jr. The limited partner is an affiliate of Great Lakes Capital Fund. Pineshores financed the project with equity from the sale of Low Income Housing Tax Credits (LIHTC), the proceeds of a 35-year HUD-insured Section 223(f) mortgage loan, and bridge loan financing provided by Capital Fund Services, Inc. The bridge loan was the lynch pin for the transaction and was required as a condition of the closing of the HUD loan.

Pineshores Apartments is an existing, 100 percent LIHTC, 120-unit family apartment complex located in Mt. Morris Township, Genesee County, Michigan. It was originally constructed in 1993 and consists of 11 two-story buildings containing 120 family units and a community building containing management, maintenance, and community laundry facilities.

The rehabilitation of Pineshores Apartments included approximately $2 million in hard costs of improvements (over $16,000 per unit) to implement significant interior and exterior

$4M

CAPITAL MAGNET FUND AWARD

renovations, all intended to reduce ongoing maintenance expenses and maintain/enhance the long-term marketability of the complex.

Construction commenced in January 2012, and was completed in June 2012, six months ahead of schedule, all with minimal or no resident relocation. The bridge loan was fully paid following the completion of construction and the promised tax credits were timely delivered.

About Great Lakes Capital Fund Nonprofit Housing Corporation (GLCF): The Great Lakes Capital Fund Nonprofit Housing Corporation was established in 1993 and operates in Michigan, Indiana, Illinois, Upstate New York, and Wisconsin. GLCF is a designated community development financial institution that invests chiefly in housing created through the federal Low Income Housing Tax Credit. GLCF also provides access to other financial resources and technical assistance through its lending arm, Capital Fund Services, and is a Fannie Mae delegated underwriter and servicer. GLCF's "One Stop Shopping" program enables developers to access permanent debt financing, construction lending, equity investment, technical assistance, and predevelopment loans through a single proposal. GLCF also operates a New Market Tax Credit portfolio and sources investments in state historic and brownfield tax credits.

FOR MORE INFORMATION
ABOUT THE IMPACT OF CDFIs
ACROSS THE COUNTRY,
VISIT **WWW.CDFIFUND.GOV**

MICHIGAN

Broderick-Murray Apartments

A CAPITAL MAGNET FUND PROJECT

SOUTHWEST HOUSING SOLUTIONS CORPORATION

The Broderick-Murray Apartments is a 36-unit residential project located in Southwest Detroit. The construction will ensure compliance with all codes and include the Enterprise Green substantial rehabilitation standards for every unit and community space. Each home will feature a washer and dryer, and these laundry facilities will be made available to all tenants at no additional cost.

The Broderick building will contain seven one-bedroom apartments, including a manager's apartment unit, and 22 two-bedroom units.

Within 350 feet of the Broderick, the Murray is located at the northwest corner of Hubbard and Porter Streets, and it features seven three-bedroom town homes. The balance of the units at the Broderick and all of the Murray town homes will be set aside for individuals earning 30 percent to 60 percent of the area median income pursuant to the Michigan State Housing Development Authority's Low Income Targeting Point Calculation Form.

The town homes will be developed under a "lease-to-own" strategy that will allow each unit to be sold to its occupant, or qualified other, at the end of the 15-year compliance period. Sale prices for each unit will be equal to the amount of outstanding debt and will also be based on appraised values. The entire lower level of the Broderick will be developed for community space to be enjoyed by residents

$2M

CAPITAL MAGNET FUND AWARD

and will feature an exercise room, kitchen and dining area, and several rooms ideal for crafts, job training, studying, and gatherings. The lower level will also feature areas for residents to store large items.

Southwest Housing and Southwest Counseling believe that for housing development to achieve success there must be a positive increase in meaningful economic and community developments including education, job training, health, culture, and similar quality of life issues. Southwest Solutions operates the following facilities in Southwest Detroit:

- 5716 Wellness (also known as The Family Wellness Center)
- Waterman Adult Facility – Southwest Counseling Adult Outpatient Center
- Adult Learning Lab
- Housing Opportunity Center and Earn and Learn Programs
- Lithuanian Hall – Southwest Housing's Property Management Department
- Campbell Branch Library
- Creative Arts Center

About Southwest Housing Solutions: Southwest Housing Solutions began in 1979 and is a leader in the planning, development, and management of affordable housing and commercial property in southwest Detroit, Michigan. Its mission is to revitalize its community through collaborative, innovative, and high-quality projects, and by promoting homeownership. Southwest Housing Solutions provides housing to low- and moderate-income residents, including persons with mental illness and the homeless. Southwest Housing Solutions stimulates commercial and cultural development through mixed-use projects and also develops and implements neighborhood preservation initiatives.

FOR MORE INFORMATION ABOUT THE IMPACT OF CDFIs ACROSS THE COUNTRY, VISIT **WWW.CDFIFUND.GOV**

MICHIGAN

5716 Wellness

A CAPITAL MAGNET FUND PROJECT

SOUTHWEST HOUSING SOLUTIONS CORPORATION

5716 Wellness was designed to meet the needs of families with young children and adolescents who are looking for ways to improve the quality of their lives and ensure their children have health care and social support. Southwest Housing Solutions Corporation is using the interest from a $600,000 Capital Magnet Fund loan to finance a much-needed parking lot for 5716 Wellness.

5716 Wellness is strategically located on Michigan Avenue (Detroit), a major thoroughfare with bus lines, in the midst of densely populated, underserved, and economically struggling neighborhoods.

The surrounding community has Detroit's highest proportion of families with young children. 5716 Wellness was created to be a convenient, accessible place for family health and wellness programming, with bilingual services available at each of the six charitable organizations that provide services in the building.

One year into this venture, more than 15,000 families have come to 5716 to receive early childhood, primary care, dental, educational, and counseling services. The partner organizations – Children's Outreach, Covenant Community Care, Life Directions, Madonna University, Moms and Babes Too, and Southwest Solutions–continue to plan collaboratively to ensure that families who come to the center

$2M
CAPITAL MAGNET FUND AWARD

About Southwest Housing Solutions:

Southwest Housing Solutions began in 1979 and is a leader in the planning, development, and management of affordable housing and commercial property in southwest Detroit, Michigan. Its mission is to revitalize its community through collaborative, innovative, and high-quality projects, and by promoting homeownership. Southwest Housing Solutions provides housing to low- and moderate-income residents, including persons with mental illness and the homeless. Southwest Housing Solutions stimulates commercial and cultural development through mixed-use projects and also develops and implements neighborhood preservation initiatives.

learn about and access all the services that are available at 5716 Wellness. Because of feedback from families that the availability of multiple services is a key benefit, the organizations are working to improve cross-agency referrals through adoption of shared values, co-location of staff, training and outreach opportunities, and resource fairs. Four of the organizations are currently either building capacity or expanding services in and around 5716 Wellness.

Other highlights of the first year of operation include:

- The organizations have worked together to leverage over $600,000 in additional funding to increase the scope of services at 5716 Wellness and improve access to services.

- One of the region's first integrated primary and behavioral healthcare programs for children has enabled Southwest Solutions to help twice as many families have access to primary care and has resulted in 30 percent of families utilizing the services of multiple agencies.

- The agencies are working together to create joint operating principles and to fund a child care program for families with young children to use while participating in services at 5716 Wellness.

- Each of the five agencies has reached or exceeded its anticipated goals.

- 5716 Wellness services are provided by 129 full-time and 32 part-time employees; nearly one-third of these positions were created as a direct result of the center.

- In recognition of the transformative and entrepreneurial nature of the project, Governor Rick Snyder awarded Southwest Solutions and 5716 Wellness the "Reinventing Michigan Award." 5716 Wellness was the first nonprofit entity in the State to be so recognized.

- O'Brien Construction Company, the contractor who performed the 5716 renovations and build-out, received the Associated General Contractors of Michigan's "Build Michigan Award,"the State's most prestigious awards in the construction industry.

FOR MORE INFORMATION ABOUT THE IMPACT OF CDFIs ACROSS THE COUNTRY, VISIT WWW.CDFIFUND.GOV

MICHIGAN

Mack Ashland LDHA LP

A CAPITAL MAGNET FUND PROJECT

SOUTHWEST HOUSING SOLUTIONS CORPORATION

Mack Ashland LDHA LP is a 39-unit new construction multiple-story building that offers permanent supportive housing to individuals and families who have special needs or are homeless. The one-acre site, located at the northwest corner of Mack and Ashland Avenues in Detroit, Michigan, is an ideal location. A full-service shopping center is located across the street, and the Northeast Guidance Center (NEGC) is located in close proximity.

NEGC will be the project's social service provider. NEGC provides behavioral health care to 4,000 residents who have mental health diagnoses. The Detroit Community Health Connection, which provides primary health care, will soon offer integrated health care at NEGC's facility located at 2900 Connor Street, Detroit.

Mack Ashland LDHA LP is situated on three parcels that are zoned Planned Development that permits a multiple story residential building with community space located on the first floor.

The project was developed and built by Southwest Housing Solutions Corporation. Mack Ashland LDHA LP has acquired site control of the properties. Mack-Ashland achieved

90

$2M

CAPITAL MAGNET FUND AWARD

"Southwest Housing Solutions Corporation is using the interest from a $600,000 Capital Magnet Fund loan to finance a much-needed parking lot for 5716 Wellness, a family wellness center in Detroit, Michigan. The parking lot will be completed by November of 2013."

Janay Mallett
Real Estate Development Specialist
Southwest Housing Solutions Corporation

a 2012 Enterprise Green New Construction Certification. The construction ensured compliance with all codes and includes the following:

- Independent forced air heat with central air conditioning for each unit;
- Energy efficient windows;
- Kitchens with wood cabinets, plastic laminate counters, garbage disposal, vinyl floor, and and energy efficient appliances including dishwashers;
- Wall-to-wall carpeting; and
- Bathrooms with ceramic tile floors and tub surrounds.

The apartment building was completed in mid-July of 2013. The building is 100 percent occupied.

About Southwest Housing Solutions: Southwest Housing Solutions began in 1979 and is a leader in the planning, development, and management of affordable housing and commercial property in southwest Detroit, Michigan. Its mission is to revitalize its community through collaborative, innovative, and high-quality projects, and by promoting homeownership. Southwest Housing Solutions provides housing to low- and moderate-income residents, including persons with mental illness and the homeless. Southwest Housing Solutions stimulates commercial and cultural development through mixed-use projects and also develops and implements neighborhood preservation initiatives.

FOR MORE INFORMATION
ABOUT THE IMPACT OF CDFIs
ACROSS THE COUNTRY,
VISIT WWW.CDFIFUND.GOV

MICHIGAN

McKinistry Place

A CAPITAL MAGNET FUND PROJECT

SOUTHWEST HOUSING SOLUTIONS CORPORATION

McKinistry Place is a 25-unit project located in Southwest Detroit. Eight two-bedroom town home units will be reserved as permanent supportive housing. The project will also include six attached town home units (three-bedrooms) and 11 single-family homes (three bedrooms).

This project was submitted to the Michigan State Housing Development Authority on August 15, 2013. Southwest Housing Solutions Corporation hopes to receive a low income housing tax credit reservation by December of 2013 to begin the project.

The construction will ensure compliance with all codes, including a Green Enterprise Certification. Each home at McKinistry Place will include the following: independent forced air heat with central air conditioning for each unit; energy efficient windows; kitchens with wood cabinets, plastic laminate counters, garbage disposals, vinyl floors, and stainless steel/double bowl sinks, and Energy Star appliances; hardwood floors; new bathrooms with ceramic tile tubs with tile surrounds. Each home will feature a washer and dryer, and these laundry facilities will be made available to all tenants at no additional cost.

$2M

CAPITAL MAGNET FUND AWARD

"Southwest Housing Solutions Corporation would not have been able to complete any of the projects without the Capital Magnet Fund award. There is no other type of funding like it for affordable housing."

Janay Mallett
Real Estate Development Specialist
Southwest Housing Solutions Corporation

The town homes will be developed under a "lease-to-own" strategy that will allow each unit to be sold to its occupant, or qualified other, at the end of the 15-year compliance period. Sale prices for each unit will be equal to the amount of outstanding debt and will also be based on appraised values.

Upon the completion of McKinistry Place, Southwest Housing Solutions and Southwest Counseling Solutions will create the following permanent positions.

- 1/4 full-time property manager;
- 1/2 full-time maintenance;
- 1/4 full-time compliance and leasing specialist;
- 1/4 full-time accountant; and
- 1/4 full-time social worker.

About Southwest Housing Solutions: Southwest Housing Solutions began in 1979 and is a leader in the planning, development, and management of affordable housing and commercial property in southwest Detroit, Michigan. Its mission is to revitalize its community through collaborative, innovative, and high-quality projects, and by promoting homeownership. Southwest Housing Solutions provides housing to low- and moderate-income residents, including persons with mental illness and the homeless. Southwest Housing Solutions stimulates commercial and cultural development through mixed-use projects and also develops and implements neighborhood preservation initiatives.

FOR MORE INFORMATION ABOUT THE IMPACT OF CDFIs ACROSS THE COUNTRY, VISIT WWW.CDFIFUND.GOV

MICHIGAN

Scotten Park

A CAPITAL MAGNET FUND PROJECT

SOUTHWEST HOUSING SOLUTIONS CORPORATION

Scotten Park is a 32-unit project located in Southwest Detroit. Eight two-bedroom town home units are reserved as permanent supportive housing. The project also includes 31 attached town home units (three-bedrooms) and one single family home (three bedrooms). The building sites are located in a concentrated area bounded by Toledo Avenue on the north; Lansing Avenue on the west; Bagley and Howard Streets to the south; and 18th Street on the east.

Southwest Housing Solutions Corporation developed Scotten Park and all of the town homes are completed and fully occupied. The construction ensures compliance with all codes, has received a 2012 Green Enterprise Certification, and includes the following:

- Independent forced air heat with central air conditioning for each unit;
- Energy efficient windows;
- Kitchens with wood cabinets, plastic laminate counters, garbage disposals, vinyl floors, and stainless steel/double bowl sinks, and Energy Star appliances;
- Wall-to-wall carpeting; and
- New bathrooms with ceramic tile tubs with tile surrounds.

$2M
CAPITAL MAGNET FUND AWARD

"Southwest Housing Solutions Corporation would not have been able to complete any of the projects without the Capital Magnet Fund award. There is no other type of funding like it for affordable housing."

Janay Mallett
Real Estate Development Specialist
Southwest Housing Solutions Corporation

Each home also features a washer and dryer, and these laundry facilities were made available to all tenants at no additional cost.

The townhomes were developed under a "lease-to-own" strategy that allows each unit to be sold to its occupant, or qualified other, at the end of the 15-year compliance period. Sale prices for each unit will be equal to the amount of outstanding debt and will also be based on appraised values.

About Southwest Housing Solutions: Southwest Housing Solutions began in 1979 and is a leader in the planning, development, and management of affordable housing and commercial property in southwest Detroit, Michigan. Its mission is to revitalize its community through collaborative, innovative, and high-quality projects, and by promoting homeownership. Southwest Housing Solutions provides housing to low- and moderate-income residents, including persons with mental illness and the homeless. Southwest Housing Solutions stimulates commercial and cultural development through mixed-use projects and also develops and implements neighborhood preservation initiatives.

FOR MORE INFORMATION ABOUT THE IMPACT OF CDFIs ACROSS THE COUNTRY, VISIT WWW.CDFIFUND.GOV

MICHIGAN

Delta River Senior Village

A CAPITAL MAGNET FUND PROJECT

VOLUNTEERS OF AMERICA NATIONAL SERVICES

Principally funded through HUD's Section 202 Program for the elderly and a grant of $287,427 through the Capital Magnet Fund, Delta River Senior Village in Lansing, Michigan is newly constructed community that provides affordable housing in 38 units to seniors 62 years of age and older.

Specifically designed to support aging in place, features include emergency call systems, non-slip floor surfaces, and grab bars.

With rents based on 30 percent of adjusted gross monthly income and significant energy saving design features, residents are relieved of a high rent and energy cost burden.

The Capital Magnet Fund (CMF) program supports financing for the preservation, rehabilitation, or purchase of affordable housing for low-income communities and community service facilities such as day care centers, workforce development centers, and health care clinics. Projects financed using the Capital Magnet Funds have had a significant impact on reducing the lack of affordable housing in the communities in which they are located.

CAPITAL MAGNET FUND AWARD

"All of the projects we have financed using the Capital Magnet Fund award have had a significant impact on reducing the lack of affordable housing in the communities in which they are located. Whether it be senior housing in Sheridan, Wyoming, family housing in Anchorage, Alaska or permanent supportive housing in Denver, Colorado, none of these very needed properties would have been developed or acquired, ensuring long-term affordability for the residents of those communities."

Patrick Sheridan
Senior Vice President of Housing Development
Volunteers of America National Services

About Volunteer of America National Services (VOANS):
Volunteers of America National Services is a subsidiary of Volunteers of America, a national faith-based organization founded in 1896 that is dedicated to helping those in need through comprehensive programs including housing and health care. Volunteers of America helps more than 2.5 million people in over 400 communities in 46 states as well as the District of Columbia and Puerto Rico. The organization supports and empowers America's most vulnerable groups, including veterans, at-risk youth, the frail elderly, men and women returning from prison, homeless individuals and families, people with disabilities, and those recovering from addictions.

FOR MORE INFORMATION ABOUT THE IMPACT OF CDFIs ACROSS THE COUNTRY, VISIT WWW.CDFIFUND.GOV

MISSISSIPPI

Holly Hills Apartments

A CAPITAL MAGNET FUND PROJECT

HOPE ENTERPRISE CORPORATION

Stratford Manor, an aging 96-unit apartment complex in Jackson, Mississippi, had fallen into disrepair. Living conditions were substandard, yet residents faced unjustifiably high rent payments. As a result, occupancy had dropped below 50 percent.

New Horizons Development, LLC, saw an opportunity to revitalize the complex and breathe new life into the neighborhood. Hope Enterprise Corporation (HOPE) provided financing for New Horizons to purchase the property, rebuild it to higher standards, and rent the renamed Holly Hills apartments to low-income families at a lower rate than they had previously been paying.

The $7.75 million Holly Hills project was made possible with funding from the Mississippi Low-Income Housing Tax Credit Equity Fund (MSEF). Managed by HOPE, MSEF is a dollar-for-dollar tax credit available for affordable housing development. Residents must meet income and other eligibility requirements.

Four local investors purchased tax credits for the project: Trustmark Bank, BankPlus, First Commercial Bank, and a local insurance company. HOPE established a partnership with Great Lakes Capital Fund (another Capital Magnet Fund awardee) to manage the compliance and underwriting of the equity fund.

$4M

CAPITAL MAGNET FUND AWARD

"William Bynum and Hope Credit Union (HOPE) won the 2013 McNulty Prize that recognizes the spirit of innovation and excellence of private sector leaders. Since 2008, HOPE has expanded from three to 15 branches; increased its member-owners from 9,000 to 28,000; and closed more than 7,200 consumer, mortgage, and small business loans totaling more than $260 million. HOPE is working to double the number of people and places it serves in "bank deserts" in the region. The John P. McNulty Prize is given annually to honor the visionary work of an Aspen Global Leadership Network Fellow of the Aspen Institute."

This was more than just a renovation," said New Horizons President and CEO Luis Jurney. "We totally gutted the complex and replaced everything." The cramped one- and two-bedroom units were replaced with 60 well-appointed two- and three-bedroom apartments to attract more families. The new units are environmentally friendly, energy efficient, and feature a host of amenities, including washers and dryers in every unit. To further enhance the living environment, old buildings were torn down and replaced with beautiful green spaces, a pool, a playground and a community center. A business center outfitted with computers and fax machines gives residents Internet access and a place to conduct personal business. "It's also a great place for children to do their homework," Jurney added.

Holly Hills officially opened in November 2011. Within two months, all units had been leased. While the standard of living has risen dramatically, the cost of living in the complex hasn't. Rents are very reasonable, and residents save money in expenses as a result of the energy-efficient design of the new units.

"This development has not only changed the face of the neighborhood, it has improved the quality of life for Holly Hills residents," Jurney said. "Today, residents live in a safe, family oriented community that they can be proud to call home."

About Hope Enterprise Corporation (HOPE): Hope is a private, nonprofit CDFI, that provides commercial financing, mortgage loans, and technical assistance to support businesses, entrepreneurs, homebuyers, and community development projects. HOPE's mission is to strengthen communities, build assets, and improve lives of people in economically distressed areas of Arkansas, Louisiana, Mississippi, and Tennessee. Since 1994, HOPE has generated over $1.7 billion in financing for entrepreneurs, homebuyers, and community development projects, and assisted more than 400,000 individuals in low-income communities throughout the Mid South.

FOR MORE INFORMATION ABOUT THE IMPACT OF CDFIs ACROSS THE COUNTRY, VISIT WWW.CDFIFUND.GOV

Santa Barbara Palms

A CAPITAL MAGNET FUND PROJECT

IDAHO-NEVADA CDFI, INC.

Through the 1990s, as Las Vegas experienced a rapid influx of a diverse population including a large retirement community, George Gekakis Inc. (GGI) recognized the need for alternative senior housing. GGI began the acquisition of appropriate sites to design, develop, build, and manage senior housing communities. Those developments now include five affordable senior rental housing community addresses. The Idaho-Nevada CDFI, Inc. financed three of these projects, the most recent Santa Barbara Palms, which is helping to meet the ever increasing need for affordable senior housing in Las Vegas, Nevada.

At Santa Barbara Palms, 72 units of affordable senior rental housing began construction in April 2011, the first phase of a 114-unit community. Configured with two-bedroom units of 978 square feet, this complex adds much needed affordable housing to the east side of the Las Vegas Valley, at the corner of Tropicana Avenue and Santa Barbara Street, just west of the US 95/515 Highway. The site is located in a mature neighborhood where area residents can age-in-place. Retail, banking, grocery shopping, medical offices, and public transportation are all close at hand.

$1.9M
CAPITAL MAGNET FUND AWARD

This project won the National Association of Home Builder's Best Of 50+ Housing Gold Achievement Award for "On-the Boards" Affordable Rental Category.

Funding for this project included GGI receiving a 9 percent Low Income Housing Tax Credit allocation from the Nevada Housing Division, Clark County HOME Funds, FHLB Affordable Housing Program Funds, and a permanent loan provided by the Idaho-Nevada CDFI.

About the Idaho-Nevada Community Development Financial Institution, Inc.: The Idaho-Nevada CDFI, Inc. was founded in 1999 to provide financing to small businesses and affordable housing entrepreneurs in the intermountain west. The Idaho-Nevada CDFI, Inc. has a primary market of Idaho and Nevada. However, on a case-by-case basis it will consider projects in other western states having distinct community development impact. Idaho-Nevada CDFI, Inc. provides financing to both for-profit and nonprofit organizations. The CDFI has found that a combination of targeted, project-specific technical assistance and low-interest financing is required by nonprofit housing developers and small businesses to move projects along in a timely manner and ensure a high-quality viable project.

FOR MORE INFORMATION ABOUT THE IMPACT OF CDFIs ACROSS THE COUNTRY, VISIT WWW.CDFIFUND.GOV

NEVADA

River Senior Apartments

A CAPITAL MAGNET FUND PROJECT

IDAHO-NEVADA CDFI, INC.

The demand for affordable senior housing in Reno, Nevada continues to grow. River Senior LLC sought to build additional housing to meet this demand and financing by the Idaho-Nevada CDFI, Inc. completed the funding package.

River Senior Apartments, a 55-unit senior affordable housing complex built in June 2011 is in a neighborhood located in the north central portion of Reno. Immediately to the north is the Truckee River green belt with an attractive bike/walking paved path. The complex is located within one-half mile from the community's largest hospital complex and is immediately west of the new AAA professional baseball stadium development.

The facility includes a computer room with free Internet access, library, and community room with kitchen, fitness room, an exam room for on-site medical screenings and office space for onsite management. Each unit includes full-size washers and dryers, patio/balcony space, locked private storage, ceiling fans, and high energy heating and cooling systems. Kitchens are equipped with full-sized refrigerators, dishwashers, garbage disposals, and oven/ranges with hoods.

$1.9M
CAPITAL MAGNET FUND AWARD

"Capital Magnet Fund cash allowed us to finance several hundred units of affordable housing that would have otherwise been beyond our capacity."

Dr. Chuck Prince
Executive Vice-President and Chief Operating Officer
Idaho-Nevada CDFI, Inc.

This is the seventh affordable development undertaken by the development team of Community Service Agency Development Corporation, and partners Robert Nielsen, Zeke Griffin, and Ann Harrington. The National Equity Fund is the Limited Partner and purchased the project's Low Income Housing Tax Credits. Other sources of funding include HOME Funds, Nevada Housing Division Exchange Funds, and the Idaho-Nevada CDFI's permanent loan.

About the Idaho-Nevada Community Development Financial Institution, Inc.: The Idaho-Nevada CDFI, Inc. was founded in 1999 to provide financing to small businesses and affordable housing entrepreneurs in the intermountain west. The Idaho-Nevada CDFI, Inc. has a primary market of Idaho and Nevada. However, on a case-by-case basis it will consider projects in other western states having distinct community development impact. Idaho-Nevada CDFI, Inc. provides financing to both for-profit and nonprofit organizations. The CDFI has found that a combination of targeted, project-specific technical assistance and low-interest financing is required by nonprofit housing developers and small businesses to move projects along in a timely manner and ensure a high-quality viable project.

FOR MORE INFORMATION ABOUT THE IMPACT OF CDFIs ACROSS THE COUNTRY, VISIT **WWW.CDFIFUND.GOV**

Welcome Home Loans

A CAPITAL MAGNET FUND PROJECT

NEW HAMPSHIRE COMMUNITY LOAN FUND

One moment in April 2011 turned the lives of Sara Cloutier and Carlos Roman Gonzalez upside down.

The couple, in their late 20s, lost a dear friend and their home when Sara found their landlord dead from a heart attack. He was like family to Sara, who had rented from him since she was 18. He had wanted to sell Sara and Carlos the house in Bethlehem, New Hampshire and they had saved for a year to make that happen.

But that moment changed everything. Their landlord's family put the house on the market. Sara was haunted by the memory of finding her friend dead. Carlos was so dejected that he sometimes just sat in his car in the driveway. They needed to move, soon, and clung to the dream of getting their own place.

"We weren't looking for an $180,000 home," Sara said. "We just wanted to be happy. We just wanted our kids to be happy and settled." It wasn't that simple. Several years earlier, not long after he moved here, Carlos's Social Security number was stolen and used to run up credit card debt. And Sara, who worked when she could at a local bed and breakfast, was getting increasingly ill; she would soon be diagnosed with Parkinson's disease.

AHEAD, an affordable housing education and development nonprofit in New Hampshire's North Country, helped the couple repair Carlos's

$3.7M
CAPITAL MAGNET FUND AWARD

"Many of the investments we made helped people find homeownership opportunities while living within their means in hard times. The Capital Magnet Fund also enabled us to structure some financing packages that allowed strong projects to get "unstuck" and move forward with important public health and environmental safety projects for low-income neighborhoods (mainly, manufactured-housing parks)."

Juliana Eades
President
New Hampshire Community Loan Fund

credit. Sara qualified for partial disability payments. The couple began looking at homes.

Time dragged. Getting bank approval for a loan would take six months, if they were approved at all. They loved two houses they saw, but just couldn't get answers.

By the time they discovered the New Hampshire Community Loan Fund's Welcome Home Loans (funded in part by a Capital Magnet Fund award), they were discouraged and skeptical. Welcome Home Loans are the nation's first real mortgage loans for owners of manufactured homes located in resident-owned communities or on their own land. They are designed for people whose modest incomes and problems with their credit history may disqualify them for traditional mortgage loans.

Just three months after their first phone call, they were in a brand-new manufactured home in Rambling Woods Cooperative, around the corner from Sara's mother, and paying just $30 more each month than they had for rent. The cooperative was happy to fill an empty lot.

"The whole way through, everybody was great. They treated us with respect," says Sara. Adds Carlos, "It was like going to a store and getting what you want, you know? 'You guys want this, you're going to get it.' It was fast."

About New Hampshire Community Loan Fund: The New Hampshire Community Loan Fund provides the financing and educational tools people need to own homes, have quality jobs and child care, and become financially independent. Established in 1983 in Concord, New Hampshire, the New Hampshire Community Loan Fund was one of the first CDFIs in the United States. The New Hampshire Community Loan Fund has loaned more than $150 million to thousands of New Hampshire individuals, organizations, and employers. Nearly every project is a collaboration with a variety of donors and lenders, including banks, credit unions, as well as other businesses, nonprofits, and government partners.

FOR MORE INFORMATION ABOUT THE IMPACT OF CDFIs ACROSS THE COUNTRY, VISIT WWW.CDFIFUND.GOV

OHIO

Eastway Village

A CAPITAL MAGNET FUND PROJECT

OHIO CAPITAL FINANCE CORPORATION

Ohio Capital Finance Corporation provided Eastway Village with a $1,020,000 loan from its Capital Magnet Fund award to cover construction costs and bridge a portion of the investor's equity.

The 66-unit new construction development consists of one- and two-bedroom apartments designed to address a critical need for affordable senior housing options in the inner-ring housing markets of Columbus, Ohio.

The 36 one-bedroom apartments are located in a two-story elevator building and will meet the needs of older, frailer seniors of which 20 of the 36 units will be restricted to seniors earning less than 40 percent of the area median income.

Additionally, the Columbus Metropolitan Housing Authority is providing 20 Project-Based Section 8 vouchers to Eastway Village.

The remaining 30 units in the project will be two-bedroom apartments arranged in six cottage buildings comprised of four and seven units each spread across the campus. This mix of unit types is intended to promote a blended community that achieves multiple goals.

$5M

CAPITAL MAGNET FUND AWARD

"The Capital Magnet Fund award has been very useful as it provided a much-needed source of low-cost capital that does not exist in the market place. The Ohio Capital Finance Corporation utilized its CMF award to provide low-cost bridge loans to Low Income Housing Tax Credit projects, thus reducing an affordable housing project's total development cost while creating housing affordable to those earning well below 60 percent of the area median income."

Jon Welty
Executive Director
Ohio Capital Finance Corporation

About Ohio Capital Finance Corporation (OCFC): OCFC is the lending arm of the Ohio Capital Corporation for Housing (OCCH). OCFC was created in 2002 to further expand OCCH's predevelopment lending activities. In May 2010, OCFC, with the assistance of the Ohio Housing Finance Agency, created the Ohio Preservation Loan Fund. The Preservation Loan Fund is designed to provide developers and owners of existing affordable housing with the tools necessary to allow the refinance and transfer of ownership while continuing the use of ongoing rental subsidies. OCFC is using its Capital Magnet Fund award to leverage investor equity in affordable housing transactions. OCFC offers products that are necessary, especially for nonprofit developers, and that generally are not otherwise available. OCFC lending permits developers to gain site control, engage engineering and environmental studies, hire architects and attorneys, conduct market studies, package projects for construction and permanent financing, as well as the acquisition of land and/or buildings for affordable housing development.

FOR MORE INFORMATION ABOUT THE IMPACT OF CDFIs ACROSS THE COUNTRY, VISIT WWW.CDFIFUND.GOV

OHIO

Abigail Apartments

A CAPITAL MAGNET FUND PROJECT

OHIO CAPITAL FINANCE CORPORATION

Ohio Capital Finance Corporation provided a loan to purchase construction materials for the Abigain Apartments project in Cincinatti, Ohio. The proceeds reduced the overall construction costs of the project since they were advanced at 0.05 percent, which is significantly less than the usual construction loan interest rate of approximately 3.25 percent.

Abigail Apartments is a scattered site project located in the Pendleton community that will consist of the rehabilitation of 70 units located in approximately 14 buildings in the Pendleton and Over-the-Rhine neighborhoods.

This development is important for the Cincinnati's urban core.

$5M

CAPITAL MAGNET FUND AWARD

"The Capital Magnet Fund award has been very useful as it provided a much-needed source of low-cost capital that does not exist in the market place. The Ohio Capital Finance Corporation utilized its CMF award to provide low-cost bridge loans to Low Income Housing Tax Credit projects, thus reducing an affordable housing project's total development cost while creating housing affordable to those earning well below 60 percent of the area median income."

Jon Welty
Executive Director
Ohio Capital Finance Corporation

About Ohio Capital Finance Corporation (OCFC): OCFC is the lending arm of the Ohio Capital Corporation for Housing (OCCH). OCFC was created in 2002 to further expand OCCH's predevelopment lending activities. In May 2010, OCFC, with the assistance of the Ohio Housing Finance Agency, created the Ohio Preservation Loan Fund. The Preservation Loan Fund is designed to provide developers and owners of existing affordable housing with the tools necessary to allow the refinance and transfer of ownership while continuing the use of ongoing rental subsidies. OCFC is using its Capital Magnet Fund award to leverage investor equity in affordable housing transactions. OCFC offers products that are necessary, especially for nonprofit developers, and that generally are not otherwise available. OCFC lending permits developers to gain site control, engage engineering and environmental studies, hire architects and attorneys, conduct market studies, package projects for construction and permanent financing, as well as the acquisition of land and/or buildings for affordable housing development.

FOR MORE INFORMATION ABOUT THE IMPACT OF CDFIs ACROSS THE COUNTRY, VISIT WWW.CDFIFUND.GOV

High Valley Estates Apartments

A CAPITAL MAGNET FUND PROJECT

NORTHWEST REAL ESTATE CAPITAL CORP.

High Valley Estates Apartments is located in Klamath Falls, Oregon. The property is located in an established area of Klamath Falls where residential development is moderate. Commercial developments are located along major thoroughfares.

Financing for the rehabilitation was completed on December 27, 2012, and began in January 2013. PNC Real Estate is the tax credit equity investor and JP Morgan Chase is the construction and permanent loan lender. Oregon Housing and Community Services is providing grant funds for the project through their Housing Development Grant and Low-Income Weatherization programs.

Exterior and site work on High Valley Estates Apartments included upgraded landscaping and perimeter fencing, new site lighting and improving/replacing existing site lighting, improved crawlspace venting, repairs/replacement of concrete sidewalk, an improved accessible sidewalk route, new drainage trenches to capture water runoff, surface asphalt repair, sealing, and striping, repair and painting of existing exterior siding, replacement of exterior windows and doors with new high efficiency exterior doors and vinyl windows, new composite shingle roofing, three new exterior stairways with new metal guards and handrails, new composite decks with metal guard

110

$5M

CAPITAL MAGNET FUND AWARD

"Our preservation of existing low-income housing is largely a rural community endeavor. In many instances our renovation of the local low-income apartment complex is the first new substantial investment in housing the community has seen for some time, so it generates a lot of local support and appreciation from the community, particularly the police, schools, and local government officials."

Brad A. Elg
President
Northwest Real Estate Capital Corp.

rails at upper units, new accessible dumpsters and enclosures, and expanded common laundry facilities with an accessible common use restroom.

The interior rehabilitation included new carpet and plank vinyl flooring, replacing kitchen appliances where necessary with new energy-star appliances, new cabinetry and countertops in all kitchens, new vanities, tubs, and tub surrounds in bathrooms, replacing most water heaters, replacing all baseboard heaters and thermostats, new smoke detectors in all bedrooms, safety improvements to guardrails at interior stairways, converting two units to meet ADA accessibility requirements, and converting one unit to meet audio/visual-impaired tenant requirements.

About Northwest Real Estate Capital Corp.: Northwest Real Estate Capital Corp. was formed in 1999. It is a regional tax-exempt affordable housing preservation company headquartered in Boise, Idaho. Since inception, the company has acquired, financed, rehabilitated, preserved, and manages over $130 million of new and existing multi-family housing in the Northwest, benefiting low-income families, the elderly, and disabled persons with incomes below 40 percent of the adjusted median income. The company's preservation activities include most types of federally regulated housing, including HUD Section 8, 202, 236, 811, Home, Section 42, USDA Section 515, and related affordable housing programs.

FOR MORE INFORMATION
ABOUT THE IMPACT OF CDFIs
ACROSS THE COUNTRY,
VISIT **WWW.CDFIFUND.GOV**

PENNSYLVANIA

60th Street Commercial Corridor, West Philadelphia

A CAPITAL MAGNET FUND PROJECT

THE REINVESTMENT FUND

The Reinvestment Fund (TRF) recently closed on a $6.7 million construction loan to support the substantial rehabilitation of 45 properties located along the 60th Street commercial corridor in West Philadelphia, using $1.65 million of its Capital Magnet Fund Award. Development will take place on the six blocks south of the 60th and Market Street Southeastern Pennsylvania Transportation Authority (SEPTA) station—the third busiest station in the SEPTA system.

While the immediate area has a solid residential base and is one West Philadelphia's historic neighborhood shopping centers, the commercial corridor is in considerable need of reinvestment. This project will repair vacant properties and build new mixed-use properties on vacant parcels. The development should have a significant revitalizing and stabilizing effect on the corridor and surrounding neighborhood.

The project will create 60 units of affordable rental housing and 15,728 square feet of commercial store-front space. The commercial properties will be below the Low Income Housing Tax Credit residential units, and will be consolidated on the first three blocks south of the train station.

CAPITAL MAGNET FUND AWARD

The developer, Neighborhood Restorations, LP (NRLP), has a proven record of leasing residential properties in the West Philadelphia rental market where there is strong demand for quality, affordable housing. All residential units will be rent restricted to those at or below 60 percent area median income, and rents will be offered below market rates for superior quality properties compared to others in the area. Units will include washers and dryers, central air, full kitchen amenities, security systems, private yards, basements, and low cost Internet services. As with the recent NRLP projects, all residential units are to be LEED certified.

About The Reinvestment Fund (TRF): TRF is a Community Development Financial Institution (CDFI) that manages over $700 million in capital and has made over $1.2 billion in community investments, financing over 2,750 projects since its inception in 1985. In pursuit of its mission, TRF finances community businesses using loan, equity, and other financing tools. TRF supports its financing with a strong research and policy analysis capacity that has become a highly regarded source of unbiased information for public officials and private investors. TRF's analytical strength is also reflected in its national online data and mapping tool that is available for all internet users at www.policymap.com. The tool offers thousands of data indicators to help users understand a place, compare places, or track investments in a place.

FOR MORE INFORMATION ABOUT THE IMPACT OF CDFIs ACROSS THE COUNTRY, VISIT WWW.CDFIFUND.GOV

RHODE ISLAND

LaCasa at Rodman Commons

A CAPITAL MAGNET FUND PROJECT

WOMEN'S DEVELOPMENT CORPORATION

The LaCasa at Rodman Commons is a project of the Women's Development Corporation in Providence, Rhode Island. The construction of 20 units of elderly housing at the LaCasa Apartment site, South Kingstown, Rhode Island was started in September 2011. Residents moved in December 2012.

There are 70 affordable senior apartments at this site. La Casa at Rodman Commons was funded under the U.S. Department of Housing and Urban Development's (HUD) 202 program and with Capital Magnet Fund capital.

The Capital Magnet Fund program supports financing for the preservation, rehabilitation, or purchase of affordable housing for low-income communities and community service facilities such as day care centers, workforce development centers, and health care clinics. Projects financed using the Capital Magnet Funds have had a significant impact on reducing the lack of affordable housing in the communities in which they are located.

$1M
CAPITAL MAGNET FUND AWARD

"The Capital Magnet Fund award was key to leveraging the funds that were invested in the completion of the project dubbed LaCasa at Rodman Commons. The Capital Magnet Fund award was both the first and final brick in the second stage of this affordable housing initiative."

Susan Aitcheson
Vice President
Women's Development Corporation

About the Women's Development Corporation (Wdc): Wdc a leader in the design, development and production of housing for low-income families, elderly and groups with special needs. In 1979, Wdc was founded by professional women with expertise in architecture and design, project and property management, community planning, historic preservation, and neighborhood development. Wdc staff consists of women and men dedicated to providing excellence in design and thoughtfulness in building, through which they strengthen communities and lives. Federal, state, and private financing allows Wdc to produce safe, desirable, and permanent housing for Rhode Island cities and towns. With these funds, Wdc preserves and restores historic buildings, constructs new, environmentally responsible housing and revitalizes neighborhoods. Wdc also serves as an impetus for economic development by enhancing tax revenues for cities and towns and creating local construction and management jobs.

FOR MORE INFORMATION ABOUT THE IMPACT OF CDFIs ACROSS THE COUNTRY, VISIT **WWW.CDFIFUND.GOV**

RHODE ISLAND

Cardinal Lane Condominiums

A CAPITAL MAGNET FUND PROJECT

WOMEN'S DEVELOPMENT CORPORATION

Cardinal Lane Condominiums is located at The Ridge of Hopkinton Meadows. It is part of a new community of 10 duplex buildings located in a beautiful park-like setting off of RI Rte 3 and Hopkinton Hill Road in Hopkinton, Rhode Island.

These 20 units, designed in the townhouse style, are made for comfortable family living and contain two bedrooms, 1.5 bathrooms, an eat-in kitchen with generous cabinets and pantry storage, a living room with space for an entertainment center, a full basement, and individual entrances and driveways with parking for two cars. The total square footage of finished living space is approximately 1,250 square feet; the basement provides an additional 600 square feet for storage.

Each duplex meets Energy Star Standards, has a very efficient, quiet heat pump system. Additional features include:

- Spacious kitchen with natural daylight and door to rear yard;
- Traditional colonial exterior design with modern interior;
- Elegant 9 foot ceilings on first floor;

CAPITAL MAGNET FUND AWARD

- Large basement;
- Large size energy efficient windows – 60 inches high;
- Coat closet, pantry closet, and large bedroom closets; and
- Washer/dryer hook up on the second floor.

About the Women's Development Corporation (Wdc): Wdc a leader in the design, development and production of housing for low-income families, elderly and groups with special needs. In 1979, Wdc was founded by professional women with expertise in architecture and design, project and property management, community planning, historic preservation and neighborhood development. Wdc staff consists of women and men dedicated to providing excellence in design and thoughtfulness in building, through which they strengthen communities and lives. Federal, state, and private financing allows Wdc to produce safe, desirable and permanent housing for Rhode Island cities and towns. With these funds, Wdc preserves and restores historic buildings, constructs new, environmentally responsible housing and revitalizes neighborhoods. Wdc also serves as an impetus for economic development by enhancing tax revenues for cities and towns and creating local construction and management jobs.

FOR MORE INFORMATION ABOUT THE IMPACT OF CDFIs ACROSS THE COUNTRY, VISIT WWW.CDFIFUND.GOV

The Villages at Cypress
A CAPITAL MAGNET FUND PROJECT

LOW INCOME INVESTMENT FUND

Just outside of Houston, Texas, the Low Income Investment Fund (LIIF) is working to help transform a seven-acre vacant parcel into 146 units of affordable senior housing.

LIIF provided AMCAL Housing, an established for-profit developer, with $1.4 million in acquisition financing to purchase the development site. LIIF's financing was supported with $1 million in credit enhancement from the Capital Magnet Fund.

The new housing development, The Villages at Cypress, will consist of eight buildings with units available to seniors earning between 30 percent and 60 percent of area median income.

Additionally, the project will include a 6,600 square-foot community center that features a library, theater, business center, an activity room, and community services space, encouraging social and physical activity for residents. The Villages at Cypress marks LIIF's first affordable housing loan in Texas. AMCAL has repaid this loan and started construction on the project.

$6M

CAPITAL MAGNET FUND AWARD

"LIIF's Capital Magnet Fund (CMF) award has enabled our organization to invest in high impact affordable housing projects, ultimately increasing the stability and well-being of low-income families. LIIF has fully deployed its $6 million CMF allocation, which has created or preserved more than 1,200 homes for families and kids, leveraged more than $120 million in private investment, created $740 million in social value and served more than 15,000 people. With funds already repaid from the original deployment, LIIF will continue to use its CFM funds for ongoing impact in distressed communities nationwide."

Nancy O. Andrews
President and CEO
Low Income Investment Fund

The CMF is providing credit enhancement so LIIF can lend in places that it has previously not done much lending, thus helping to invest in communities that are underserved by CDFIs. CMF's ability to absorb risk and provide favorable terms have supported LIIF's growth into new geographies, infusing more community development capital into markets. To date, LIIF has used CMF capital to credit enhance projects in Houston, Texas and Denver, Colorado, two new markets for the organization.

About the Low Income Investment Fund: As a leading national community development financial institution, LIIF invests capital in low-income people and communities. Since its founding in 1984, LIIF has invested $1.3 billion in projects serving highly distressed neighborhoods. Through its financing and technical assistance, LIIF has served 1.4 million people and generated $25 billion in family and societal benefits.

FOR MORE INFORMATION ABOUT THE IMPACT OF CDFIs ACROSS THE COUNTRY, VISIT WWW.CDFIFUND.GOV

WISCONSIN

Access Dental Facility

A CAPITAL MAGNET FUND PROJECT

FORWARD COMMUNITY INVESTMENT

Forward Community Investments (FCI), a cerfitied CDFI, provided economic development in addition to affordable housing with its Capital Magnet Fund (CMF) award. An example is a dental facility in Dodgeville, Wisconsin by Southwestern Wisconsin Community Action Program (SWCAP). The facility was expanded to include a 4,100 square foot dental clinic with eight units, a waiting room reception area, and offices to provide services for low-income families from throughout Iowa County. It primarily serves people who are on Medicaid, and other low-income people are served on a sliding scale.

"Access currently operates a four-chair dental clinic in Dodgeville, but this new building will allow them to more than double their capacity," said Wally Orzechowski, executive director of SWCAP. "The current dental clinic has been used to capacity and has a waiting list." Lack of accessible dental care for low-income families is always one of the highest reported local needs identified in surveys done by SWCAP.

Every three years, SWCAP does a Community Needs Assessment providing updated demographic data and community information. It helps identify the strengths, needs, and trends that impact the design and implementation of SWCAP's various programs.

$3.8M
CAPITAL MAGNET FUND AWARD

"The Capital Magnet Fund was especially useful because the majority of the projects funded with CMF dollars were in rural communities. These are the communities that sometimes have the hardest to finance projects because simply getting the projects to closure is a small feat in itself."

Salli Martyniak
President
Forward Community Investments

"FCI is delighted to be participating in such a wonderful project that will continue to deliver the much needed health access to the low-income individuals in Iowa and surrounding counties," said Salli Martyniak, president of FCI. "FCI's long-standing partnership with SWCAP is a prime example of nonprofits working together to strengthen communities, provide jobs, and deliver services to those in need throughout the region."

Because this was an expansion project that included several partners with little to no discretionary cash or cash flow to collateralize the loan, traditional lenders were hesitant to fund the project. Yet, this "difficult to finance" project has provided amazing results according to Wally Orzechowski, Executive Director, "This is an example of what FCI loans can do to solve or at least mitigate a social problem. The numbers for Dodgeville alone are 1,385 unique patients seen and 4,058 encounters in 2012."

About Forward Community Investments (FCI): FCI transforms communities by supporting projects and programs that focus on affordable housing, job creation, economic development, and basic social services. Whether it's through one-on-one advising or workshops, FCI works with nonprofit managers to assess their organization's financial and organizational condition and help them appreciate their strengths and opportunities and manage areas of financial weakness – all for the purpose of increasing programmatic effectiveness and expanding the opportunity for greater social impact. FCI offers a variety of workshops, webinars, and one-on-one advising that are designed to build its clients' capacity, grow their financial effectiveness, and improve their social impact. FCI provides money and expert advisory services to nonprofit organizations serving communities most in need. Since 1994, Forward Community Investments has lent more than $25 million to nonprofits across Wisconsin. These loans have created and sustained more than 1,200 units of affordable homes, provided affordable childcare for about 1,500 children, and created or retained 3,100 jobs.

FOR MORE INFORMATION ABOUT THE IMPACT OF CDFIs ACROSS THE COUNTRY, VISIT WWW.CDFIFUND.GOV

WISCONSIN

The Fountains of West Allis
A CAPITAL MAGNET FUND PROJECT
GREAT LAKES CAPITAL FUND NONPROFIT HOUSING CORPORATION

The Fountains of West Allis is a 35-unit Section 8 property for disabled individuals. The majority of the residents have sight and physical disabilities.

The rehabilitation of the property included flooring, cabinets, countertops, painting, plumbing, light fixtures, and air conditioning (not previously provided). Exterior improvements included windows, roof, asphalt, landscaping, and a fenced-in area for guide dogs. Common area improvements included flooring, painting, updated elevator, ADA signage, auto entry door, light fixtures, computers with readers for those with sight disabilities. The improvements clearly made a substantial improvement in the quality of life for the residents that call The Fountains home.

Funding for the acquisition and rehabilitation of the property was made possible by a Low Income Housing Tax Credit investment, a pre-development loan provided by the Great Lakes Capital Fund through the Capital Magnet Fund, and permanent financing provided by the Great Lakes Capital Fund. There are very few options for affordable housing available for individuals with disabilities in the Milwaukee area. The property has maintained 100 percent occupancy and currently has a one-year waiting list.

$4M

CAPITAL MAGNET FUND AWARD

Great Lakes Capital Fund Nonprofit Housing Corporation has used all of its initial Capital Magnet Fund award and has been able to reinvest the money into an acquisition loan for a property in Indiana, a construction loan on a development in Wisconsin, and a predevelopment loan for a development in Indiana.

About Great Lakes Capital Fund Nonprofit Housing Corporation (GLCF): The Great Lakes Capital Fund Nonprofit Housing Corporation was established in 1993 and operates in Michigan, Indiana, Illinois, Upstate New York, and Wisconsin. GLCF is a designated CDFI that invests chiefly in housing created through the federal Low Income Housing Tax Credit. GLCF also provides access to other financial resources and technical assistance through its lending arm, Capital Fund Services, and is a Fannie Mae delegated underwriter and servicer. GLCF's "One Stop Shopping" program enables developers to access permanent debt financing, construction lending, equity investment, technical assistance, and predevelopment loans through a single proposal. GLCF also operates a New Market Tax Credit portfolio and sources investments in state historic and brownfield tax credits.

FOR MORE INFORMATION ABOUT THE IMPACT OF CDFIs ACROSS THE COUNTRY, VISIT **WWW.CDFIFUND.GOV**

For more information about the CDFI Fund:

Website: www.cdfifund.gov

Phone: (202) 653-0300

Mailing Address: U.S. Department of the Treasury
Community Development Financial
Institutions Fund
1500 Pennsylvania Avenue, NW
Washington, DC 20220

Office Address: U.S. Department of the Treasury
Community Development Financial
Institutions Fund
1801 L Street, NW
6th Floor
Washington, DC 20036

www.ingramcontent.com/pod-product-compliance
Lightning Source LLC
Chambersburg PA
CBHW080300290526
45790CB00005B/1874